T0308624

Regional Implications of an Independent Kurdistan

Alireza Nader, Larry Hanauer, Brenna Allen, Ali G. Scotten

For more information on this publication, visit www.rand.org/t/RR1452

Library of Congress Cataloging-in-Publication Data is available for this publication.
ISBN: 978-0-8330-9569-5

Published by the RAND Corporation, Santa Monica, Calif.
© Copyright 2016 RAND Corporation
RAND® is a registered trademark.

Cover: Beneath the Kurdistan flag, Kurdish Peshmerga troops keep watch in northern Iraq near the border with Syria (Azad Lashkari/Reuters).

Support RAND
Make a tax-deductible charitable contribution at
www.rand.org/giving/contribute

www.rand.org

Preface

In this report, we examine the potential regional implications of an independent Kurdistan in Northern Iraq. Specifically, we examine the possible reactions of the three key neighbors: the rest of Iraq, Turkey, and Iran. We closely analyze scenarios in which an independent Kurdistan might emerge and various policy options available to Baghdad, Ankara, and Tehran. However, we do not predict that an independent Kurdistan will emerge, nor do we advocate for an independent Kurdistan. Rather, we examine the implications of such a possibility for the region.

Funding for this study was provided, in part, by donors and by the independent research and development provisions of RAND's contracts for the operation of its U.S. Department of Defense federally funded research and development centers. The research was conducted within the RAND National Security Research Division (NSRD) of the RAND Corporation. NSRD conducts research and analysis on defense and national security topics for the U.S. and allied defense, foreign policy, homeland security, and intelligence communities and foundations and other nongovernmental organizations that support defense and national security analysis.

For more information on the RAND National Security Research Division, see www.rand.org/nsrd/ or contact the director (contact information is provided on the web page).

Contents

Figures

Summary

In this report, we examine the potential regional implications of an independent Kurdistan in northern Iraq. Specifically, we analyze the interests of key three regional neighbors—the Iraqi central government, Turkey, and Iran—and explore policies each actor may pursue in response to Kurdish independence. However, we do not recommend an independent Kurdistan in northern Iraq or anywhere else.

The question of Kurdish independence has been raised—by academics, by third countries, and by Kurdish leaders themselves—since the Kurds established a semi-autonomous region in the wake of the first Gulf War. Since the overthrow of Saddam Hussein, Iraqi Kurdish leaders worked diligently to maximize their control over affairs in the north, and tensions between Baghdad and the Kurdish Regional Government (KRG) in Erbil—particularly regarding the distribution of resources and control over oil and disputed territories—have led many Kurdish officials to take steps that further distance the KRG from the central Iraqi government. Kurdish officials have long complained that the KRG does not get its fair share of resources from Baghdad, and several senior Kurdish leaders have stated bluntly that independence is their eventual goal.

As a result, the question of whether Iraqi Kurdistan may someday become a sovereign country is not merely theoretical; it is a very real possibility whose impact on regional dynamics should be assessed. In this report, we do not predict that an independent Kurdish state will actually emerge, either in northern Iraq or elsewhere, nor do we advocate for an independent Kurdish state. Rather, we examine the likely implications for the region if the KRG were at some point to declare its secession from Iraq.

U.S. policy toward the Middle East is currently focused on the Islamic State in Iraq and the Levant (ISIL) and the humanitarian crisis in Syria. Not as much attention is paid to the relatively stable KRG of northern Iraq, which one day could emerge as an independent Kurdistan, with important consequences for regional stability and U.S. national security.

The KRG has in some ways operated as a de facto Kurdish state since the implementation of a U.S.-led no-fly zone in 1991 curtailed Baghdad's influence in the north. Iraq's post-Saddam constitution institutionalized the Kurdistan Region's political and economic autonomy. The emergence of an independent Kurdistan has been strongly opposed by the Iraqi central government and has been seen as a threat to the interests of major regional states, including Iran and Turkey, both of which have sizable Kurdish populations that have advocated for greater political and cultural rights. Recent regional developments, however, have led to some major changes in attitudes toward the Iraqi Kurds.

Although Baghdad has vigorously objected to an independent Kurdistan, it may not have enough leverage to prevent such an outcome, although the Iraqi central government could complicate the Kurdish drive for independence.

Turkey has come to see some benefit in a stable and more autonomous Kurdistan. The KRG is now Turkey's second-biggest export market after Germany and an increasing source of oil for Turkey's economy. A stable and prosperous Iraqi Kurdistan Region could also serve as a counterweight to the emergence of an autonomous Kurdish zone in Syria, which Turkey strongly opposes.

Iran may be wary of an independent Kurdistan that could stir its own repressed Kurdish population, but it also maintains solid ties with the KRG and may view it as a valuable ally against the avowedly anti-Shi'a Islamic State.

In general, the reaction of Baghdad, Ankara, and Tehran to Kurdish independence will depend on the scenarios under which the KRG becomes independent. In this report, we examine three such scenarios: a unilateral declaration of Kurdish independence that is broadly opposed by the region, a "last man standing" scenario in which the Iraqi state collapses and the KRG becomes an independent state, and a gradual estrangement between Erbil and Baghdad. We also consider how each of these scenarios could be influenced by a resurgence of Kurdish nationalism in which—whether encouraged by Iraqi Kurds or not—Kurdish populations in Iran, Turkey, or Syria not only support the establishment of a sovereign Kurdistan in northern Iraq, but even seek to join the new nation.

As far as the United States is concerned, regional reactions to an independent Kurdistan may not produce greater instability in the region if Kurdish independence takes place in a gradual manner or, ideally, comes as a result of negotiations between Baghdad and Erbil. Turkey is likely to welcome an independent Kurdistan under such a scenario, and Iran may tolerate Kurdish independence if it does not lead to greater instability within Iran's borders. The Iraqi central government may be the most likely to oppose an independent Kurdistan, but it may have little choice but to accept an independent Kurdish state, given its weakened position.

We make the following conclusions for each key regional actor.

Iraq

The Kurds in northern Iraq have struggled to gain independence for nearly a century. From the perspective of Iraq's central government, the secession of the Kurds would pose a direct challenge to Baghdad's authority. These conflicting interests are a constant undercurrent in Baghdad-Erbil relations and are the cause of several ongoing political disputes: the status of Iraq's disputed territories, sharing the federal budget, and Kurdish oil development.

The Kurdish Region currently consists of the provinces of Dohuk, Erbil, and Sulaimaniyah, as well as large sections of land known as the "disputed territories": ethnically mixed territory claimed by both Erbil and Baghdad. The Kurds gained control of much of the disputed territories, including the oil-rich governorate of Kirkuk, in 2014, and were the Kurdistan Region to become independent, it is likely that Kirkuk would be part of it.

Despite Baghdad's unwavering insistence that the Kurdistan Region will remain a part of Iraq, the central government's ability to prevent the Kurds from gaining independence may be limited. Baghdad faces significant challenges that inhibit it from acting decisively to maintain control of the KRG: a weakened military struggling to regain territory from ISIL, a financial crisis, sectarian tensions and severe political divisions, a fledgling economy, and in general a sluggish recovery from decades of war. It seems unlikely that Baghdad will be able to overcome these hurdles in the near future, which limits its courses of action to oppose Kurdish sovereignty.

Though Baghdad may be unable to stop the emergence of a Kurdish state, how the central government would react to Kurdish independence depends on how such independence is gained. A unilateral declaration of Kurdish independence is likely to provoke the most hostile response from Baghdad of all the scenarios we explored in this study. The central government could see this unilateral action as an affront to Iraqi sovereignty and as a serious challenge to Baghdad's ability to keep the country united. Baghdad would also oppose Kurdish independence gained after the collapse of the Iraqi state, but would have very few courses of action available to punish the Kurds. If a gradual estrangement between Erbil and Baghdad led to a negotiated separation, Baghdad could attempt to extract as many benefits from Kurdish independence as possible while mitigating the negative impact of losing the Kurdistan Region, especially if a new Kurdish state would maintain control of Kirkuk and most of the disputed territories. Overall, Kurdish independence gained through a mutually acceptable agreement between Baghdad and Erbil has the most possible benefits for both parties of all the scenarios examined in this study.

Baghdad's response should also be viewed in a regional context. The effect of Baghdad's response to Kurdish independence could be augmented if Baghdad had the ability to work with other powers, namely Iran or Turkey. The impact of any economic or military action Baghdad could take would be strengthened if coordinated with the regimes in Tehran or Ankara. This cooperation would be most likely to occur if Kurdish independence was accompanied by the reemergence of pan-Kurdish nationalism and leadership, which Turkey and Iran would view as a threat to their domestic interests.

The KRG would likely consider the response of Baghdad to Kurdish independence before seeking to break away from Iraq. There are several factors that could influence Baghdad's reaction and the effectiveness of a response. The Kurds would face significant challenges in their effort to establish sovereignty, and managing Baghdad's reaction is one of many issues the KRG would need to consider.

Turkey

Ankara may accept the eventual existence of a sovereign Kurdish state in what is now northern Iraq, depending on circumstances, although the means by which such a state may come about could affect the extent of Turkey's initial support.

Turkey has abandoned its long opposition to Iraqi Kurdish independence for a number of reasons stemming from Turkey's internal politics, Turkey's energy needs and economic imperatives, and growing political uncertainty in Iraq and Syria.

Perhaps first and foremost, before the recent resumption of violence between Ankara and the Kurdistan Workers' Party (PKK), the Turkish government had made a political decision to resolve its conflict with Turkish Kurds, agreeing to permit Kurds to mobilize politically and advocate for social and cultural rights. Civilian Turkish governments stopped viewing political mobilization by Turkish Kurds as a threat to the state, as previous military-dominated regimes once did, and Turkish Kurdish leaders abandoned their pursuit of an autonomous Kurdish zone in favor of integration into Turkish politics and society. As a result of these two changes, Ankara came to stop fearing that an independent Iraqi Kurdistan would fan Kurdish separatism among its own Kurdish population. Turkey seems to have regressed on this front since violence broke out after a Kurdish-dominated party's success in June 2015 parliamentary elections denied the ruling party a majority, and a resumed counterinsurgency campaign against the PKK was undertaken principally to consolidate the government's power through new parliamentary elections, which were held in November 2015. A July 2016 coup attempt against the Erdoğan government led to further crackdowns on local Kurdish officials and educators, whom the government tied to the exiled politician it claimed masterminded the coup attempt. These anti-Kurdish measures, too, were designed to strengthen the central government's power rather than to reignite the anti-Kurdish culture wars. Although the parliamentary elections and the coup attempt did drive the Turkish government to take steps to enhance its domestic authority, neither the resumption of violence nor the coup attempt appears to have changed Ankara's strategic calculus regarding Iraqi Kurdish independence.

Second, years of Turkish investment and trade in Iraqi Kurdistan have transformed the KRG into an increasingly important economic partner. At the same time, the rapid growth of the Turkish economy overall has driven Turkey to import more oil and gas and to seek to diversify its energy supplies. The prospect of increased access to Iraqi Kurdish oil and gas[1] (not to mention the prospect of additional transit fees) has made Erbil a valued energy partner for Turkey as well.

Third, Ankara would no longer view Kurdish independence as a driver of Iraq's collapse and thus a harbinger for violence and instability along its border. Turkey distrusts the Shi'a-dominated government in Baghdad, which—in addition to being heavily influenced by Iran—has proven unable to deflect ISIL, maintain security, or facilitate energy exports. Ankara views the KRG as more likely than Baghdad to promote stability on Turkey's border.

Fourth, Turkey has become extremely concerned that Syrian Kurds aligned with the PKK will establish an autonomous zone along Turkey's southern border from which the PKK could resume an anti-Turkish insurgency if peace talks fail. While Turkey is working to undermine the Syrian Kurds in a number of ways—including, in mid-2016, through direct military intervention—it has tried to

---

[1] In 2013, Turkey and the KRG agreed to construct new pipelines with the capacity to export 2 million barrels of oil per day (bbl/d) and 10 billion cubic meters (bcm) of natural gas per day from the Kurdistan Region to Turkey (Pamuk and Coskun, 2013).

influence Syrian Kurdish behavior by working through Iraqi Kurdish leaders.

The KRG has gradually increased its ability to act as a de facto state, and Turkey has encouraged this dynamic (and its slow pace) through similarly gradual increases in political contacts, commercial investment and trade, and oil purchases. Ankara would likely endorse a sovereign Kurdish state that has moved gradually toward independence or that has broken away from an Iraqi state collapsing from internal squabbles and violence. However, abrupt actions by the Iraqi Kurds to change the status quo could cause Turkish leaders to pull back. They might fear, for example, that an unexpected declaration of independence by the KRG would signal that Iraqi Kurds intended to claim the mantle of Kurdish nationalism and promote greater autonomy among Kurds in Turkey and Syria. Similarly, they might fear that the KRG's sudden secession could prompt Baghdad to cut off diplomatic relations and trade with Turkey if Ankara chooses to endorse a Kurdish state; although Turkish trade with Iraq's central government is not enormous, Ankara may not want to cut off the possibility of importing oil from southern Iraq if and when the southern portions of the Iraq-Turkey pipeline come back online. From Turkey's vantage point, slow and steady progress toward Kurdish independence has significant political and economic advantages, whereas sudden moves toward sovereignty pose political and economic risks.

Iran

The Islamic Republic's reaction to an independent Kurdish state will be influenced by the state of relations with its own Kurdish population as well as its perception regarding the intentions of outside powers. The issue of an independent Kurdistan is sensitive for the Islamic Republic because of fears that it would embolden its own large population of repressed Kurds.

While Iranian Kurds would welcome the emergence of an independent Kurdistan in northern Iraq, the extent of the connection they felt to it likely would vary, depending on multiple factors ranging from tribal, linguistic, and religious affiliation to geographic location within Iran to political ideology. Kurds are not a monolithic group, with important differences existing both across national borders and among communities inside each country. Widespread and public celebrations of Kurdish independence inside Iran would likely heighten Tehran's threat perception, resulting in crackdowns at home and a more aggressive stance toward the new Kurdish state.

Iran's assessment of its contemporary geopolitical position relative to its rivals would greatly influence its reaction to Kurdish independence. Iranian elites are divided over what impact Kurdish independence would have on Iran. Some are concerned that a partitioned Iraq could weaken the Islamic Republic's regional position; with three small countries resulting from fragmentation, outside powers would find it easier to manipulate each one. Others believe that Iran can benefit from an independent Kurdistan that has good relations with Tehran. Washington's end goal regarding the Kurds is a source of debate in Tehran. Some believe U.S. statements that it does not support the creation of an independent Kurdistan, while others argue that the United States wants to break Iraq up into "bite-sized" pieces that could be more easily dominated. The reaction of NATO member Turkey, which has recently increased its influence over the KRG, would also shape Iran's course of action following Kurdish independence.

Iran's economic ties to the KRG could temper its reaction to Erbil's declaration of independence, especially if Turkey decides to continue increasing its market share among the Kurds. That Iran has increased its economic ties to the KRG despite Baghdad's strong objections indicates that financial benefits may ultimately outweigh Iranian concerns over Kurdish nationalism. So while Iran may not be entirely happy with Kurdish independence, it might hesitate to react violently to an independent Kurdistan.

The manner in which Erbil declares independence will affect Iran's threat perception, thus greatly determining Tehran's reaction. If Kurdish independence were to occur, the best scenario for the Iranians would be one in which independence follows drawn-out discussions with Baghdad, which would provide time and the political environment for Tehran to adopt a pragmatic policy that could adjust to a new neighboring state as well as temper Iranian Kurdish attraction to a new state, specifically through domestic economic development and political reforms. On the other hand, a unilateral and abrupt announcement of Kurdish independence likely would empower Iranian hawks, who see Iran's Kurdish situation solely through a security lens, sidelining pragmatists in the government who would prefer to address the challenge by improving the lives of Iran's minorities. Harsh crackdowns on Kurds celebrating Erbil's action likely would reinforce Kurdish nationalism in Iran. Similarly, if Iraq were to become a failed state, with Iran increasingly responsible for protecting the Baghdad government, conservative factions would hold sway over Tehran's policy toward the Kurds. In all scenarios, Iran would react harshly if Kurdish independence in northern Iraq was followed by Erbil espousing pan-Kurdish nationalism.

The successful implementation of a nuclear deal between Iran and the P5+1 (United States, Russia, China, United Kingdom, France, and Germany) could hold implications for Tehran's outlook on the Kurdish issue. An Iran relieved of sanctions would be free to intensify its investments in a new Kurdish state, likely focusing on the energy industry, as well as construction of a rail network to further integrate the two economies. In the event that the nuclear agreement falls apart, conservatives in Iran likely will succeed in sidelining pragmatists in Tehran, lessening the chance that Iranian Kurdish grievances will be addressed.

Acknowledgments

The idea for this report emerged from informal discussions among RAND staff regarding the myriad changes affecting the Middle East and the "wild card" events—such as Kurdish independence—that could dramatically change regional dynamics. Charles Ries, Howard Shatz, and Robin Meili of RAND provided useful suggestions about how to scope the research questions for an examination of such a hypothetical development. RAND's Seth Jones helped to ensure that the research methodology was both rigorous and clearly explained. Linda Robinson of RAND and Gönül Tol of the Middle East Institute, who served as peer reviewers, offered valuable insights that improved the report's arguments and enhanced its usefulness for analysts and policymakers.

CHAPTER ONE

Introduction

The United States has focused much of its attention and efforts in the Middle East on reaching and implementing a nuclear deal with Iran while countering the rise of the Islamic State of Iraq and Levant (ISIL). Relatively little attention has been paid to a potential—maybe even a likely—event that could have significant implications for the region and for U.S. national security interests: the prospect that the Kurdistan Regional Government (KRG) in what is now northern Iraq could declare independence.

The question of Kurdish independence has been raised—by academics, by third countries, and by Kurdish leaders themselves—since the Kurds established a de facto autonomous zone in the wake of the first Gulf War. Since the overthrow of Saddam Hussein, Iraqi Kurdish leaders worked diligently to maximize their control over affairs in the north, and tensions between Baghdad and the KRG in Erbil—particularly regarding the distribution of resources and control over oil and disputed territories—have led many Kurdish officials to take steps that further distance the KRG from the central Iraqi government. Kurdish officials have long complained that the KRG does not get its fair share of resources from Baghdad, and several senior Kurdish leaders have stated bluntly that independence is their eventual goal.

As a result, the question of whether Iraqi Kurdistan may someday become a sovereign country is not merely theoretical; it is a very real possibility whose impact on regional dynamics should be assessed. In this report, we do not predict that an independent Kurdish state will actually emerge, either in northern Iraq or elsewhere, nor do we advocate for an independent Kurdish state. Rather, we examine the likely implications for the region if the KRG were at some point to declare its secession from Iraq. Kurdish independence could change the region dramatically. If accepted by the international community and its neighbors, it could enable the Kurdistan Region–Iraq to free itself of the political instability and financial uncertainties associated with its inclusion in the Republic of Iraq. With a relatively well-educated population, oil and gas resources that are reported to be extensive, and favorable trade and investment trends with Turkey, the KRG could be on a path to rapid political stabilization and economic development. However, the KRG's secession and the absence of the Kurds to balance the Sunni-Sh'ia rivalry could cut off the Iraqi central government's economic outlet to Turkey, further pit Sunnis and Shi'a against each other in a quest for political power and control of resources, and lead to further or complete disintegration of Iraq.

Neighboring Turkey and Iran have established close relations with Erbil over the past two decades—Ankara more so than Tehran—and could benefit from the presence of a stable, gas- and oil-exporting trade partner on their borders. However, both countries have restive Kurdish populations of their own, and both could see a successful independent Kurdistan as a force for irredentist nationalism that incites Kurdish secession movements in Turkey and Iran. Should the KRG seek statehood, the way in which it does so—and the extent to which it depends on a pan-Kurdish nationalist narrative to justify independence—could influence Turkey's and Iran's receptivity to KRG independence.

With the establishment of no-fly zones and no-drive zones following the 1991 Gulf War that prevented Saddam Hussein from extending his authority to the Kurdish areas of northern Iraq, Iraqi Kurds managed their own affairs with little interference from Baghdad for more than a decade. Although Iraqi Kurdish leaders are ambiguous about their desire for an independent state, they nevertheless methodically went about establishing its foundations, including autonomous political bodies, security forces, and institutions to manage education, health care, utilities, and the like. After the fall of Saddam, the Kurds ensured that the Transitional Administrative Law (TAL), the law establishing official government authorities prior to the implementation of a new constitution, and the constitution adopted in 2005 would protect their autonomy while leading up to a census and a referendum on the status of the disputed territories—a process called "normalization." In addition, Kurdish interests in Baghdad were protected by the selection of Jalal Talabani as president and the allocation of a deputy prime minister slot to a Kurd in the Iraqi system of ethno-sectarian balance. Yet, constitutional, legal, economic, and political disputes with the post 2005 Shi'a-dominated governments in Baghdad prevented this process of "normalization" from moving forward, which placed Kurdish leaders in the tenuous position of pledging fealty to the central government while advocating for the right to claim territory the Kurds argue is historically Kurdish land.

In 2014, as the central government's control fell apart during the ISIL onslaught, KRG President Masoud Barzani declared that the collapse of Iraqi authority left the Kurds with no choice but to take their own path. Kurdish forces took control of Kirkuk and other adjacent disputed territories, the status of which had been a significant obstacle to the implementation of the normalization process. On July 1, 2014, President Barzani declared, "The goal of Kurdistan is independence,"[1] and two days later he tasked members of the Kurdistan parliament to form an electoral commission that would organize a referendum on the Kurdistan Region's independence.[2]

Yet other Kurdish officials seemed to put the brakes on this sudden move toward secession. Former Iraqi Foreign Minister Hoshyar Zebari, a Kurd, asserted in August 2014 that ISIL's advance called for independence to be "put aside . . . not abandoned," noting that "priorities have changed" because of the ISIL threat.[3] Several months later, in December 2014, KRG Deputy Prime Minister Qubad Talabani told a Washington think tank audience that Kurdistan will be independent "in our lifetimes" but cautioned that Kurdish independence must develop "as a natural progression" of politics and economics that is achieved in

---

[1] Quoted in "Iraq Kurdistan Independence Referendum Planned," 2014.

[2] "Iraq: Kurdish President Proposes Independence Referendum," 2014.

[3] "Lally Weymouth Interviews Former Iraqi Foreign Minister Hoshyar Zebari," 2014.

consultation with neighboring countries and allows the maintenance of good relations with Iraq, Iran, and Turkey.[4]

A combination of strong national identity, two decades of de facto autonomy, and a sense that Kurds would be better off running their own affairs than being tied to a disintegrating Iraqi state suggests that eventual Kurdish independence is likely. But senior Kurdish officials appear to disagree on the pace at which the KRG should pursue sovereignty, the drivers that would indicate the time is ripe, and the impact of the KRG's decision on its relations with the rest of Iraq, as well as Iran and Turkey, its key neighbors.

In this report, we do not seek to assess the KRG's internal decisionmaking dynamics to identify when, or in response to what events, the KRG might seek independence. However, we do seek to understand the range of reactions that the KRG's neighbors might have to a Kurdish declaration of independence, as these states' decisions to shun or engage a newly independent Kurdish state could either bolster or undermine its viability.

In chapters dedicated to the Iraqi central government, Turkey, and Iran, we review the history of each country's interactions with the KRG and other relevant Kurdish groups, such as the Turkish Kurdistan Workers' Party (Partiya Karkerên Kurdistanê, or PKK), the Syrian Democratic Union Party (Partiya Yekîtiya Demokrat, or YPD), and the Iranian Party for Free Life of Kurdistan (PJAK). We examine each country's political, economic, and security interests in the Kurdistan Region and how its policies have changed in response to regional events. Finally, based on a judgment that the manner in which the KRG seeks independence could affect the neighboring countries' policy responses, each chapter examines the neighbors' reactions to three scenarios, which are described below.

The report focuses on the reactions of three key regional actors that border the KRG and would be impacted by Kurdish independence in northern Iraq: the Iraqi central government in Baghdad, Turkey, and Iran. We made extensive use of primary sources, especially in Persian

---

[4] KRG Deputy Prime Minister Qubad Talabani, remarks at the Center for Strategic and International Studies, December 10, 2014.

and Turkish, and also relied on secondary sources for a description of Kurdish history and current Kurdish politics. We also attended several roundtables and conferences on Kurdish issues to inform our analysis.

The first chapter of the report offers a relatively brief historical background on the issue of Kurdish independence, the second chapter examines potential Iraqi reactions to an independent KRG, and the third and fourth chapters analyze potential Turkish and Iranian reactions, respectively. The final chapter offers conclusions.

Scenarios

We use three analytical scenarios for Kurdish independence: a unilateral declaration of independence in which the KRG announces the formation of a Kurdish state to the surprise of the international community; a last-man-standing situation in which Iraq's central government collapses, leaving the Kurds with no option but to become independent; and a gradual estrangement in which increasing Kurdish autonomy eventually leads to its separation from the rest of Iraq. These scenarios assume that independent Kurdistan includes the three provinces that are officially part of the KRG, as well as sections of the disputed territories the KRG has occupied since ISIL's advance into Iraq in the spring and summer of 2014 and Kurdish and non-Kurdish areas the peshmerga (Kurdish security forces) subsequently liberated from ISIL. According to peshmerga commanders in 2015, about 90 percent of the disputed territories are now under Kurdish control.[5] Without possession of these oil-rich territories, an independent Kurdistan might not be economically viable. The new state would have control over oil production in all areas of its territory, including the oilfields in Kirkuk province, which is one of Iraq's top-yielding governorates for oil production. Demographically, a new Kurdistan would contain a majority of Kurds as well as significant minority populations, including Arabs, Turkmens, Yazidis, Assyrians, and Chaldeans. Kurdistan's borders would touch Turkey in the north, Iran in the north and east, Syria in

---

[5] Ahmed, 2015.

the west, Baghdad-controlled Iraq in the south, and ISIL-controlled territory in the west and south.

We do not assess as a distinct scenario the continuation of the current status quo, for several reasons. First and foremost, the intention of the report is to consider whether and how the emergence of an independent Kurdish state in northern Iraq might change regional dynamics. As a result, assessing the continuation of the KRG's current status within a federal Iraq would not provide insights into questions being considered. Second, much of the analysis in the report focuses on current political, social, and economic trends, which captures fairly thoroughly the current role of the KRG in the region, thus making it unnecessary to consider a separate "null set" scenario involving no change of the KRG's status. Third, while a scenario that assumes no change in the KRG's status does not mean that the relations between Turkey, Iran, and the region's Kurds would remain unchanged in any way, such a scenario would suggest that non-Kurdish actors would be the principal drivers of any changes in regional dynamics. This, too, would fail to provide insights into the effects of a proactive Kurdish decision to seek independence.

The analytical scenarios are as follows.

1. Unilateral Declaration of Independence

The KRG declares itself an independent and sovereign nation. KRG President Masoud Barzani seeks diplomatic recognition from key allies in North America, Europe, and the Middle East and pledges to seek membership in the United Nations.

Though the announcement comes as a surprise to the international community, the factors that pushed the Kurds toward independence have been present for years. Fed up with continued disagreements with Baghdad over hydrocarbons, sharing the federal budget, the status of the disputed territories, and a lack of progress toward implementation of constitutional provisions regarding Kurdish autonomy, the KRG feels compelled to end its inclusion in the Iraqi state and to forge a future as an independent nation. Kurds across northern Iraq express their strong support for separation, while minorities in KRG-controlled territory (particularly Turkmen and Sunni Arabs) are uneasy about being in a Kurdish-dominated country. Kurds in Turkey, Syria, Iran, and in diaspora communities in Europe and the United States voice support for the new nation, but nascent indications of pan-Kurdish nationalism in the Middle East quickly fade.

Baghdad, believing the KRG's actions threaten the integrity of the Iraqi state, immediately announces its rejection of Kurdish independence, claiming that secession is illegitimate and accusing the KRG of stealing Iraqi territory and resources. Baghdad lays claim to the KRG's oil and gas resources and infrastructure, promising to retaliate against international oil companies that invest in the Kurdistan Region and to claim ownership of Kurdish oil exports in regional and international courts. The new border between Kurdistan and Iraq becomes increasingly fortified. Ankara approaches Kurdistan cautiously, as it stands to benefit from Kurdish independence but wants to avoid a backlash from Baghdad. Tehran proclaims its opposition to Kurdish independence but closely monitors the impact on its domestic Kurdish population before determining how to respond.

This scenario could occur at any time in the future. In fact, a situation similar to this looked possible in the summer of 2014, when the Kurds threatened to hold a referendum on independence shortly after seizing large sections of the disputed territories. The conditions that could make the Kurds unilaterally declare independence already exist and are unlikely to dissipate.

2. Last Man Standing

Chaos reigns in Baghdad, and the central government loses the ability to provide basic services to Iraqi citizens throughout the country. Iran exerts more and more influence over politicians in Baghdad, and the Kurds feel increasingly isolated and frustrated as long-standing disputes persist and sectarian tensions become more entrenched. ISIL continues to hold wide swaths of Iraqi territory. The Iraqi Army collapses, and Shi'a militias dominate large swaths of southern Iraq and Baghdad. Oil exports fall as Baghdad neglects energy infrastructure, and Iraq's annual revenue plummets. Without the ability to collect and disseminate revenue, Baghdad stops sending monthly payments to the

KRG. The KRG decides there is no longer anything to be gained from remaining in a failed state and declares independence.

Baghdad expresses its opposition to Kurdish independence but no longer possesses political or economic leverage over the new state. Turkey becomes one of the first nations to recognize Kurdistan and establish diplomatic ties, in part as a means of containing the instability from central Iraq, winning a commitment from KRG leaders to maintain pressure on Syrian Kurds, and ensuring its continued access to Kurdish energy resources on preferential terms. Most countries, realizing Kurdish independence is inevitable and hoping that secession will bring stability in at least one portion of what was once Iraq, provide diplomatic recognition of the new state. Tehran, however, is less enthusiastic about the emergence of the new nation.

Aspects of this scenario have been playing out in Iraq for several years. During the summer of 2014, that process accelerated as ISIL seized Iraqi territory. Despite the crisis of June and July 2014, the central government retains control of Baghdad and is pushing back ISIL's advance with Iranian and American assistance. Iraq's failure is no longer imminent, but the central government is still struggling to overcome sectarian tensions and provide services to Iraqi citizens, as well as settle long-standing disputes with the Kurds.

3. Gradual Estrangement

The KRG grows economically and politically stronger. The Kurdish oil industry is booming despite Baghdad's threats to retaliate against the buyers of Kurdish oil. The KRG has become financially self-sufficient and has developed close ties with Ankara and, to a lesser extent, Tehran. Baghdad loses leverage over the KRG, and negotiations stall over revenue sharing, oil exports, and the status of Kirkuk and other disputed territories, where the KRG is firmly entrenched. The KRG could either declare independence unilaterally or negotiate its separation with Iraq's central government. Baghdad would be motivated to enter into separation negotiations for one of two reasons: (1) Baghdad sees Kurdish independence as inevitable and decides to mitigate its losses through a negotiated settlement, or (2) Baghdad calculates that it has more to gain in the long run by facilitating Kurdish independence and developing strong bilateral relations than by opposing it and creating an adversary on its border.

The emergence of an independent Kurdistan is not a surprise. Iraq's Kurds are enthusiastic about independence, and Kurdish populations outside northern Iraq express support for the new nation. Minorities within the KRG remain suspicious of Kurdish rule, but the Kurds have used the drawn-out run-up to independence to reassure minority populations that they would have nothing to fear from a Kurd-dominated political system—particularly given that they have already been living under a de facto Kurd-dominated polity for years. Baghdad's acquiescence to an amicable divorce is well known and perhaps even encouraged by Iraq's international partners, and nations around the world recognize the new Kurdish state without fear of Iraq's retaliation. Turkey and Iran have expected for years that Kurdistan would gain sovereignty and have taken steps to alleviate the potential negative impacts this could have domestically.

This scenario takes years to develop and extends further into the future than the other scenarios described. In some ways, the groundwork for this outcome had already been laid with the 2014 agreement between Iraqi President Haider Abadi and President Barzani regarding revenue sharing and Kurdish contributions to Iraq's oil exports. The fact that an agreement was reached demonstrated new levels of Kurdish-Iraqi cooperation, but perhaps even more notable was the absence of a provision restricting Kurdish oil exports outside the exports contributed to the State Organization for Marketing of Oil (SOMO). It seems Baghdad was willing to ignore unilateral Kurdish exports it previously called illegal. However, the 2014 agreement failed, as neither side considered that the other fulfilled its obligations, and as of spring 2016 sharp differences over oil policy and revenue sharing persist.

Influence of Kurdish Nationalism

All of the above scenarios are based principally on a decision by the KRG that independence furthers the interests of Iraqi Kurds more than remaining part of a federal Iraqi state. However, the conduct and outcome of each of these scenarios could be influenced by a resurgence of Kurdish nationalism in which—whether encouraged by Iraqi Kurds or not—Kurdish populations in Iran, Turkey, or Syria not only support the establishment of a sovereign Kurdistan in northern Iraq, but even seek to join the new nation. The emergence of a Kurdish state could influence the expression of Kurdish nationalism within the borders of Turkey and Iran, generating fears in Ankara and Tehran that the new Kurdish state has irredentist intentions or could cause Kurdish secessionist movements in their own countries to gain followers and influence. Baghdad would not likely be affected significantly by the rise of pan-Kurdish nationalist sentiments, but Baghdad could take advantage of distrust in Ankara and Tehran to rally opposition in those capitals to Kurdish independence. Minorities within the KRG (for example, Arabs and Turkmen) would resist the prospects of living in a new state characterized as a Kurdish homeland rather than as a democratic state that happens to have a majority Kurdish population.

It is unlikely that current KRG President Masoud Barzani would try to encourage such a pan-Kurdish state. Over the past several years, President Barzani has not presented himself as a pan-Kurdish leader, making it less likely that an independent KRG would emerge as the center of a renewed regional Kurdish nationalism. Barzani does not support the PKK or its quest for independence from Turkey; furthermore, the KRG's political and economic dependence on Turkish support makes it unlikely that any Iraqi Kurdish leader would risk isolation from Turkey in exchange for ethnic solidarity with Turkish Kurds. Even though Barzani has provided some assistance to Syrian Kurds who are seeking to establish an autonomous Kurdish enclave in northeastern Syria—a dynamic viewed with great suspicion by Ankara—he has also expressed opposition to Syrian Kurdish independence. Although there are no indications that Barzani or any other Iraqi Kurdish leader would portray the KRG as the vanguard of pan-Kurdish nationalism, it is possible that Kurds throughout the Middle East would look to a newly independent Kurdish state as something to mimic or join.

Since each of the KRG's neighbors has long feared a resurgence of nationalist sentiment among its own Kurdish population, for each scenario we will examine the potential impact of Kurdish nationalism on the degree to which Kurdish independence might be accepted by Turkey, Iraq, and Iran.

CHAPTER TWO

Background

The Kurds of the Middle East are frequently cited as the world's largest national group without a state. Around 30 million members of the Kurdish community are spread across Iraq, Iran, Syria, and Turkey, and substantial Kurdish diaspora communities reside in Europe and the United States.[1] The Kurds share a rich culture, though they are divided between many states and continents. These previously nomadic tribes have roots dating back two millennia, and although the Kurds demonstrated some degree of group awareness by the 16th century,[2] they began seeing themselves as a community with a distinct identity only about 100 years ago.[3] The Kurds predominantly speak two major dialects, Surani and Kurmanji, and have unique cuisine, clothing, and dance, all of which contribute to a larger Kurdish identity that is distinct from Turkish, Persian, and Arab cultures. They call their homeland Kurdistan (Figure 2.1).[4] For centuries, the Ottoman Empire claimed most of this territory, and Kurdish lands were divided between the states that emerged following the Ottoman's collapse. The Kurds have been fighting to achieve independence since national borders were drawn across the Middle East nearly 100 years ago.

The turmoil that engulfs the Middle East today may provide an opportunity for the KRG to create an independent state. Iraq's frac-

---

[1] McDowall, 2003.

[2] Bozarslan, 2008, p. 336.

[3] McDowall, 2003, pp. 1–2.

[4] McDowall, 2003, p. 6.

Figure 2.1
Predominantly Kurdish Areas Overlaying Modern-Day State Borders

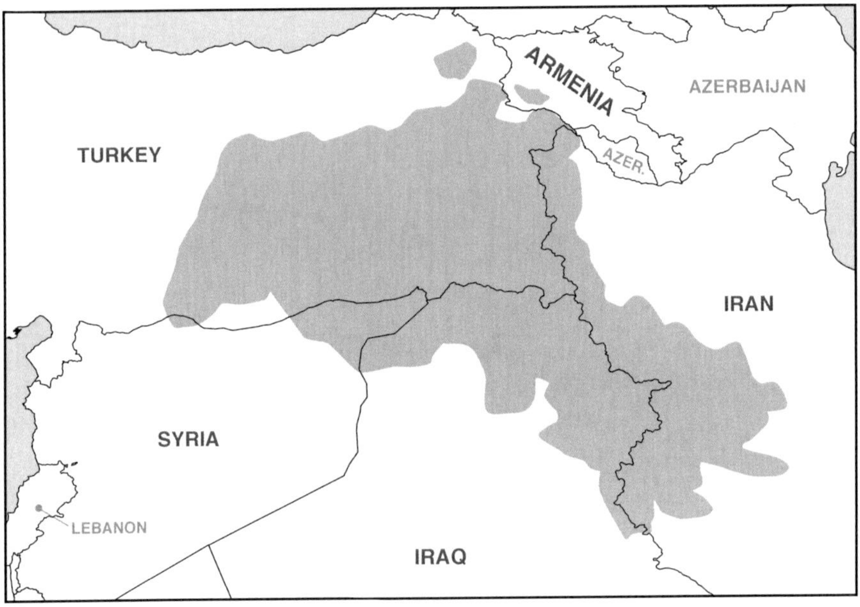

RAND *RR1452-2.1*

tured central government, driven by intra- and inter-sectarian divisions, is struggling to regain territory conquered by ISIL. The Kurdistan Region, on the other hand, appears stronger and more unified, with a vibrant economy (although it has been badly damaged by the recent oil price collapse and over 20 percent increase in its population from refugees and primarily internally displaced persons [IDPs]), a functioning regional government, and security forces largely capable of protecting Kurdish lands, albeit crucially with U.S. air support. Despite current economic difficulties, KRG leadership ushered in an extended period of economic growth through such measures as a liberal investment law (KRG Law 4 of 2006), entry visas granted at the airport without bureaucratic hassles, a liberal regime for expanding oil- and gas-related investment, and vast improvements in KRG-wide electricity provision. However, the KRG will need to overcome a legacy of divided political leadership in the region between two parties with roots in the insurgency against Saddam, and its previous inability to maintain strategic relations with regional actors, if independence is to be feasible in the future.

The Kurds and the Emergence of the Modern Middle East

After World War I, the Allied powers gathered at the Paris Peace Conference to determine new international borders for Europe, the Middle East, and Asia, which presented an opportunity for the Kurds to form their own nation. President Woodrow Wilson introduced the concept of self-determination, reflecting a new way of thinking in the international community. Wilson pushed his Fourteen Points to become the centerpiece of the peace negotiations. The twelfth point directly addressed the future of non-Turkish people living under Ottoman rule, though it fell short of promising independence: "The Turkish Portions of the present Ottoman Empire should be assured a secure sovereignty, but other nationalities which are now under Turkish rule should be assured an undoubted security of life and an absolutely unmolested *opportunity for autonomous development*" (emphasis added).[5] The concept of self-determination in the Middle East alluded to in the twelfth point conflicted with European imperial ambitions in the region that were outlined in the 1916 Sykes-Picot Agreement, in which the British and French agreed to share control of Ottoman territory at the end of the war. This agreement divided Kurdish lands between the two European powers (Figure 2.2).

A few years after the Sykes-Picot agreement was reached, Britain negotiated with France to transfer possession of the vilayet of Mosul, which was an Ottoman administrative district in what today is the northern border of Iraq. Mosul's jagged mountains created a natural border between British-controlled territory and the southern border of the Ottoman Empire.[6] Moreover, this area possessed rich wheat districts. Britain, recognizing the strategic and economic value

---

[5] Wilson, 1918.

[6] McDowall, 2003, pp. 117–121.

Figure 2.2
Map of Sykes-Picot Agreement

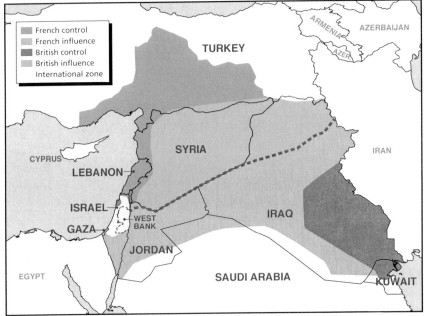

NOTE: This map superimposes British- and French-claimed territory from the Sykes-Picot Agreement over today's boundaries in the Middle East, illustrating how France and Britain's dividing of the region cut through Kurdish lands in what is today northern Iraq.
RAND *RR1452-2.2*

of acquiring Mosul and the area around it, negotiated with France to transfer this territory to British control, thus slightly altering how the Sykes-Picot agreement divided the Middle East. It was this agreement between the British and French following World War I that resulted in Iraq's northern border being drawn through the mountainous region that continues to separate northern Iraq from southern Turkey and modern-day Syria (Lekic, 2014).

The Kurds lacked a unifying figure in the post-war years that could claim to legitimately represent all Kurdish people.[7] The few lead-

---

[7] Izady, 1992, p. 59.

ers that did emerge did not have widespread support among the Kurds and in some cases alienated the British by being perceived as overly aggressive in their attempts to form an independent state. The British also failed to provide a viable alternative to the Sykes-Picot Agreement and were therefore unable to offer a clear idea of how the Kurds' future could unfold.[8] As a result, the Kurds did not have leadership capable of cooperating with Britain in reaching a political solution to the question of Kurdish independence or autonomy in 1919.

The issue of Kurdish statehood resurfaced in the 1920s as the borders of the Middle East solidified. Britain's policy on the Kurds, however, was inconsistent. The possibility of Kurdish independence was raised by the British decision to administer Iraq's Kurdish region separately from the rest of Iraq and in the Treaty of Sevres, which promised the Kurds an autonomous region that could apply to the League of Nations for independence.[9] These actions conflicted with the 1923 Treaty of Lausanne, a peace treaty between the allied powers and Turkey that did not include a provision for Kurdish independence, and with the 1924 alliance between Britain and Iraq, which was conditioned upon Britain securing Iraqi rights in Mosul.[10] In 1926, the League of Nations officially awarded control of Mosul and the territory around it to Iraq rather than to Turkey, whose previously strong Ottoman influence in Mosul had been largely erased through British efforts to reorient the province's society and economy toward Baghdad and Basra.[11] The contradictory positions the British took on Kurdish autonomy and independence throughout the early 1920s demonstrated the lack of a coherent policy toward the Kurds, and the Treaty of Lausanne and 1924 alliance closed a window of opportunity for Kurdish autonomy or independence.

---

[8] McDowall, 2003, p. 134.

[9] Izady, 1992, p. 50.

[10] McDowall, 2003, p. 143.

[11] Shields, 2009, p. 217.

The Kurds in Pre-Saddam Iraq

The inability of the Kurds to garner support from regional actors, which prevented them from establishing an independent state after World War I, continued to prevent Iraq's Kurds from achieving autonomy or independence throughout Iraq's pre-Saddam era. The Covenant of the League of Nations created the mandate system, by which territories that transferred from the control of one government to another at the end of the war and which the League deemed not ready for independence were placed under the administration and tutelage of a more advanced country.[12] It was in this way that Britain established a mandate in Iraq. Not long after the mandate was established, Britain began seeking ways to minimize its commitments in Iraq. Britain and the Iraqi monarchy negotiated an early termination of the mandate that would allow Iraq to become independent in 1932, but this treaty omitted provisions for Kurdish rights. When the terms for independence became public, prominent Kurds petitioned the League of Nations for autonomy or independence and for recognition of other Kurdish rights the government in Baghdad had failed to extend.[13] Kurdish nationalism, which had been largely dormant for several years, began spreading throughout the region, and anger over long-ignored Kurdish demands boiled over into mass demonstrations in Sulaimaniyah in September 1930. Kurdish objections to Iraq's independence under the agreed-upon terms undermined British efforts to end the mandate, as the League of Nations was unlikely to grant Iraq independence unless the Baghdad government appeared able to assume the mantle of sovereignty. Britain's desperation to end its mandate obligations prompted it to work with the Iraqi government to hide Kurdish discontent over Arab rule.[14] Ultimately, the Kurds failed to separate themselves from the rest of Iraq when independence was gained in 1932.

The Kurds made several efforts to establish relations with actors inside and outside Iraq who could promote Kurdish interests between

---

[12] League of Nations, 1919.

[13] McDowall, 2003, pp. 172–173.

[14] McDowall, 2003, p. 177.

the end of the British mandate in 1932 and the beginning of the Saddam era. A series of coups following the collapse of the Iraqi monarchy in 1958 brought into power several different governments led by military elites, Nasserists, and Ba'athists. At one time or another, the Kurds reached out to each of these groups, all of whom abandoned the Kurds when the relationship failed to serve their interests, just as the British had during the mandate period. Iran, too, proved to be a fair-weather ally during the pre-Saddam era, as Tehran withdrew support for Kurdish military operations against the central government when it became politically convenient in the mid-1970s.[15] The United States also abandoned the Kurds in the mid-1970s, opting to support peace negotiations between Iran and Iraq and cease support of Kurdish uprisings the United States had previously backed.[16]

Divided Kurdish leadership also impeded efforts to gain autonomy and independence in the pre-Saddam era. Kurds demonstrated only limited political organization in the 1930s, and Baghdad suppressed what little nascent political activity emerged.[17] In the 1940s, efforts to encourage pan-Kurdish solidarity began to take hold. In 1943, clashes between the forces of Kurdish leader Mullah Mustafa Barzani and the Iraqi military catapulted Mullah Mustafa into a position of prominence among the Kurdish population.[18] In 1946, he used his power to unite pro-Kurdish factions into one single party, the Kurdistan Democratic Party (KDP), which remains a major Kurdish political party today.[19] Although the KDP was the leading Kurdish party for several decades, the KDP's failure to maintain Iranian support and defeat government forces in the 1970s significantly weakened the party, creating a political vacuum in the Kurdish region that led to a group of KDP members splitting from the party and forming the Patriotic Union of Kurdistan

---

[15] McDowall, 2003, p. 338.

[16] Gunter, 2011, p. 96.

[17] McDowall, 2003, pp. 287–288.

[18] McDowall, 2003, p. 293.

[19] McDowall, 2003, p. 296.

(PUK) under the leadership of Jalal Talabani.[20] The KDP maintained its stronghold in the northwestern provinces of Erbil and Dohuk, while the PUK established itself in the eastern province of Sulaimaniyah, which borders Iran. Within a few years, intra-Kurdish fighting erupted as the KDP and PUK competed for influence among the population. This competition created lasting political and geographical divisions among the Iraqi Kurds that continue to undermine Kurdish efforts to attain independence.

The Kurds Under Saddam

Saddam Hussein came to power in a bloody coup in 1979. The Kurds' suffering during Saddam's reign created a common feeling of victim-hood that is now ingrained in the Kurdish identity; brought the plight of the Kurdish people to the forefront of international attention; and—by highlighting the Kurds' seeming inability to live in peace in an Arab-majority country—inspired efforts to gain independence from Baghdad. Over the course of the Iran-Iraq War from 1980 to 1988, Saddam murdered and tortured thousands of Kurdish civilians in retaliation for Kurdish efforts to subvert the Iraqi government and expand their influence internationally.[21] Saddam's ruthlessness reached genocidal levels in the spring and summer of 1988, as General Ali Hasan al Majid, known as Chemical Ali, unleashed the multi-stage Anfal campaign.[22] The March 1988 chemical attack on Halabja in particular captured international attention after news of it leaked out and made a permanent impression on the consciousness of Iraqi Kurds. Saddam continued to persecute the Kurds in the early 1990s, when he brutally repressed anti-government uprisings in the wake of the Gulf War, which caused a significant refugee crisis. The years of mass murder

---

[20] Jabary and Hira, 2013.

[21] Bozarslan, 1996, p. 100.

[22] The Anfal campaign was a multi-phase operation executed by Baghdad in 1988 to commit genocide against the Kurds. Hundreds of thousands of Kurds died as a result of chemical weapons attacks on population centers and the systemic slaughtering of any who escaped.

and destruction of Kurdish society created a common bond among Iraq's Kurdish population and have become a driving force for Kurdish independence.

The suffering of Kurdish refugees in the early 1990s attracted international attention. On April 5, 1991, the United Nations Security Council adopted Resolution 688, which condemned the attacks on all Iraqis, including the Kurds, and demanded that Saddam stop attacking civilians in areas that had revolted against his regime in the largely Kurdish north and the Shi'a south.[23] Soon thereafter, the U.S. military provided the displaced Kurds life-saving supplies and protection as they returned to their villages in a humanitarian campaign called Operation Provide Comfort.[24] After the Kurds had been safely repatriated, the U.S.-led mission provided security for civilians by enforcing a no-fly zone to prevent Iraqi military flights from entering airspace over northern Iraq. Saddam blockaded the Kurdish region after renewed autonomy negotiations with the central government collapsed.[25] The resulting economic separation from Baghdad, combined with the presence of international assistance and security provided by the no-fly zone, presented an opportunity for the Kurds to pursue de facto political and economic autonomy without significant interference from Baghdad.

In January 1992, the KDP, PUK, and other Iraqi opposition representatives met in Syria to form a government in exile, which organized an election to select a new parliament and leader in May 1992. The KDP and PUK won an almost equal number of votes, leading to a power-sharing agreement between the two parties that held until it was recently challenged by the emergence of a PUK splinter, the Gorran party. The regional parliamentary election led to the creation of the Kurdistan National Assembly (later renamed the Kurdistan Parliament) and the foundation of the KRG.[26] That government directly

---

[23] United Nations Security Council, 1991.

[24] Stewart, 2010, p. 431.

[25] McDowall, 2003, p. 378.

[26] Kurdistan Regional Government Department of Foreign Relations, 2016.

ruled over three governorates, although in the aftermath of the 2003 war, it extended its powers into additional territories over which control was disputed between Erbil, the capitol of the KRG, and Baghdad (Figure 2.3); these territories will be discussed more thoroughly in a later chapter. Ultimately, fears of violating Iraq's sovereignty and territorial integrity made outside actors reluctant to recognize or work with the KRG throughout the 1990s, undercutting the new government's authority and capabilities.[27]

Barzani and Talabani's competition for power kept the Kurds politically divided. In May 1994, a land dispute sparked hostilities between the two parties, igniting a civil war that continued on and off throughout the rest of the decade and resulted in the deaths of

Figure 2.3
Post-2003 Iraq and the Disputed Territories

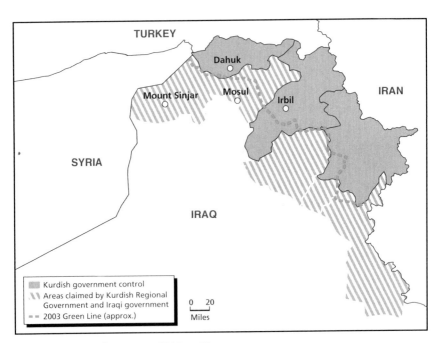

SOURCE: Adapted from Kane, 2011, p. 12.
RAND *RR1452-2.3*

---

[27] Natali, 2010, p. 35.

thousands of Kurds at the hands of other Kurds.[28] Saddam, hoping to diminish the influence of U.S.-provided military and financial assistance in the Kurdish region and reassert his authority over northern Iraq, provided heavy weaponry to the KDP; meanwhile Iran, which also hoped to undermine the U.S. role in Iraq, backed the PUK.[29] Saddam and Iran used the Kurds as pawns, and the Kurdish parties became increasingly reliant on outside support throughout the 1990s, which further contributed to the PUK and KDP's inability to reconcile their differences and unite behind their shared goal of Kurdish autonomy and independence.

In addition to the political turmoil that plagued the KRG during the 1990s, sluggish economic growth stymied the region's development. This was almost entirely due to the so-called double embargo. While the international community embargoed Iraq, including the Kurdistan Region, the rest of Iraq also embargoed the KRG. Economically isolated from Iraq and unable to establish formal economic relations with sovereign states in the region, the Kurdistan Region became dependent on a large underground economy that developed along the Turkish border.[30] Goods shipped between provinces in the northern region and between Arab and Kurdish areas were taxed by Kurdish officials. When Operation Provide Comfort ended in 1996, funds continued to flow into the Kurdish region through the Oil for Food Program (OFFP), which was controlled by the United Nations (UN) and Baghdad in such a way that few Kurds felt the benefits of this program while Saddam, the UN, and private businesses accrued interest from unspent funds.[31] When the United States toppled Saddam Hussein's regime in 2003, 60 percent of the Kurds lived below the poverty line.[32]

---

[28] McDowall, 2003, p. 386.

[29] McDowall, 2003, pp. 388–389.

[30] Natali, 2010, p. 44.

[31] Natali, 2010, pp. 54, 70–72.

[32] Natali, 2010, p. 70.

KRG-Iraqi Relations After Saddam

The U.S. invasion of Iraq provided the Kurds with a unique opportunity to influence Iraqi affairs while courting foreign actors who could help the Kurds achieve independence. The Kurds enthusiastically supported the U.S. policy of regime change in Iraq and the subsequent U.S. invasion. In late March 2003, Kurdish forces helped facilitate the parachuting of 2,100 soldiers into Bashur airfield from Aviano, Italy, and began working with American troops to fight the Iranian-based Islamic Group of Kurdistan and Ansar al-Islam, an al Qaeda affiliate.[33] After eliminating the threat from these groups, Kurdish and U.S. Special Forces turned their attention to fighting Saddam's army and the Republican Guard along the Green Line, the de facto border between the Kurdistan Region and the rest of Iraq. As the Iraqi Army disintegrated, U.S. and Kurdish forces seized cities across northern Iraq. The Kurds used this opportunity to take control of Kirkuk, the ethnically mixed and oil-rich city that Kurds view as an integral part of an independent Kurdistan.

The end of Saddam's oppressive regime and the boycott of the new government by Sunni political parties enabled the Kurds not only to participate in, but also to shape the creation of, a new Iraqi government and its subsequent policies. The Iraqi Governing Council created by the Coalition Provisional Authority (CPA) contained 25 seats for individuals representing every cross-section of Iraqi society, 20 percent of which were reserved for Kurdish leaders.[34] While the U.S. commitment to a unified Iraq prevented the Kurds from gaining independence after Saddam's fall, the Kurds used their new influence in Baghdad to negotiate bilaterally with the CPA for concessions, such as the acceptance of Kurdish as an official state language and promises to resolve disputes over Kirkuk. These concessions were included in the TAL and Iraqi Constitution.[35] Kurds also took on roles in both the interim and official governments that succeeded the CPA and the Governing

---

[33] Gordon and Trainor, 2006, pp. 340–341.

[34] Allawi, 2008, p. 164.

[35] Allawi, 2008, pp. 221–222.

Council, which has greatly enhanced their influence on political decisions made in Baghdad. Jalal Talabani, founder of the PUK, became
Iraq's new president, and Barham Saleh, another PUK leader, became
Iraq's deputy prime minister.[36] Kurds also have occupied the positions
of Army chief of staff, foreign minister, and finance minister at various
times since Iraq regained sovereignty in 2004.[37]

Despite the Kurds taking on a visible role in the central government immediately following the collapse of Saddam's regime, Kurdish
political influence began to wane soon thereafter. The Sunni boycott
of the new government ended in May 2005, and as the Sunni and
Shi'a political parties became more organized, they diluted Kurdish
influence and delayed enacting constitutional provisions that would
have granted the Kurds concessions over contentious issues.[38] Kurd-
ish-Arab tensions persist to this day. Article 140 of the constitution,
which laid out measures, including a referendum, to resolve disagreements over the disputed territories, was never implemented, in part
because of Iraqi political instability otherwise. Erbil and Baghdad still
disagree over possession of these areas, particularly the oil-rich province of Kirkuk. Disagreements between the KRG and the central government of Iraq over Kurdish oil exports and sharing the state budget
also remain an obstacle between the central and regional governments.
Years of political grievances for both Kurds and Arabs have driven a
significant wedge between the KRG and the central government, suggesting that cooperation between the two governments going forward
will be occasional at best and nearly impossible at worst.

The Current State of Intra-Kurdish Politics

Modern Kurdish politics has been defined by the competition between
the KDP and PUK. Early in the KDP's history, two factions emerged:

[36] Allawi, 2008, p. 280.

[37] Hiltermann, 2012.

[38] Brennan et al., 2013, p. 148.

one led by Mustafa Barzani and the other led by Ibrahim Ahmad.[39] In the late 1960s, Ibrahim, along with his son-in-law Jalal Talabani, split from the KDP. When Talabani formed the PUK in 1975, he sparked a decades-long competition with the Barzani family, who still control the KDP, over which party should represent the Kurds.[40] Over the past several decades, both parties have built a constituency around tribal and family loyalties rather than political ideology. Party affiliations now dominate Kurdish society, and the parties' extensive patronage networks deeply affect the professional lives of Kurds. Despite the progress the KRG has made toward attaining more autonomy since Saddam's collapse, the KDP and PUK are still far from establishing a cooperative government, and the two parties coexist peacefully while maintaining geographic separation in northern Iraq.

While the KDP-PUK struggle for influence is ongoing, the emergence of a PUK-rival party known as Gorran has disrupted the political status quo in the Kurdistan Region. This PUK splinter group, whose name means "change" in Kurdish, emerged on the KRG's political scene in 2009 and has since challenged the balance of power between the KDP and the PUK. Gorran is particularly popular in the province of Sulaimaniyah and with Kurdistan residents age 25 and below, who make up 60 percent of the KRG's population. The party has taken a strong anti-corruption stance, and its willingness to criticize the patronage system in Kurdish politics has contributed to its growing popularity. In the September 2013 elections, Gorran won more seats than the PUK in the Kurdistan Parliament, winning 24 seats to the PUK's 18. For a short period of time, Gorran representatives led some of the KRG's most powerful ministries, such as the Ministries of Finance, Peshmerga Affairs, Trade and Industry, and Endowment and Religious Affairs.[41] In October 2015, amid protests that the KDP claimed Gorran orchestrated, Prime Minister Nechirvan Barzani, a KDP leader, removed Gorran's leaders from the cabinet and KDP security forces blocked Youssef Muhammad, a Gorran leader and the

---

[39] Jabary and Hira, 2013.

[40] Gunter, 1996, pp. 242–241.

[41] Harris, 2014, p. 2.

parliamentary speaker, from entering Erbil.[42] Many of the protesters at that time were civil servants demanding that the government resume distributing salaries, while others were expressing their opposition to President Masoud Barzani's decision to serve a third term despite constitutional limitations on doing so. Since Gorran was unseated in Erbil, Gorran's leaders have entered into a political agreement with the PUK. The agreement calls for the PUK and Gorran to run on the same ballot in the 2017 elections, which could upend the PUK-KDP alliance that has been in place for decades.[43] Given the KRG's quickly changing political environment, however, the continued rapprochement between Gorran and the PUK is anything but certain.

Although Gorran's rapid rise has shaken the political system, the long-term effect of this party is not yet evident. Gorran's platform has tapped into the frustration many Kurds feel about corruption and nepotism, frustration that erupted into violent demonstrations in Sulaimaniyah from February to April 2011.[44] Various grievances motivated protesters during this period, which some called the "Kurdish Spring," but resentment of the KDP and PUK's domination of Kurdish society and government was an undercurrent. Whether Gorran can continue to harness this desire for social and political change may heavily affect its long-term viability. Furthermore, Gorran recently made some political decisions that suggest that the party is moving away from its platform to reform the political system in the KRG. Gorran made a deal with the KDP to form a new government in the spring of 2014, after which Gorran support declined in Kirkuk and Erbil.[45] Gorran also remained silent in February 2015 on the fourth anniversary of the killing of a Kurdish teen at the 2011 Sulaimaniyah demonstrations.[46] In past years, Gorran organized anti-KDP campaigns on the anniver-

---

[42] MacDiarmid, 2015.

[43] "How Does the PUK-Gorran Deal Affect Kurdish Politics?" 2016.

[44] Gunter, 2013, pp. 441–457.

[45] "Iraqi Kurdistan: Gorran Movement Popularity Decreases After Deal with Barzani's KDP," 2014.

[46] "Gorran Forgets the 4th Anniversary of Feb 17 Uprising in Iraqi Kurdistan," 2015.

sary to protest the involvement of KDP guards in the teen's death, but its silence on the issue just months after entering a political agreement with the KDP suggests that Gorran may be abandoning some of its previous positions in order to gain a political foothold in Erbil. Also, Gorran's support mostly comes from traditionally PUK areas, but the PUK has significantly more financial resources, international support, and its own PUK-peshmerga forces.[47] These resources could enable the PUK to stymie Gorran's growing influence and rebound from the internal struggles the party has faced since Jalal Talabani's influence diminished due to a stroke he suffered in 2012. Whether Gorran will maintain independence from the PUK now that the two parties appear to be cooperating is unclear. In short, Gorran's ability to offer a political alternative to the KDP and PUK may be diminishing, and its permanence in Kurdish politics is far from certain.

Iran's and Turkey's competition for influence in the KRG also affects intra-Kurdish politics, as was clear in the KDP's summer of 2014 push to gain independence. Masoud Barzani is currently the president of both the KDP and the KRG and has close ties with Turkey. Turkish foreign policy elites—who often evoke the memory of the Ottoman Empire and espouse the benefits of expanding Turkish influence in former Ottoman territory—may refrain from blocking a Kurdish bid for independence in the belief that Ankara's ties to Barzani and the KDP give Turkey an opportunity to exert influence over a Kurdish nation.[48] While the KDP was actively discussing holding a referendum on independence in the summer of 2014, which would have included Kurdish areas such as Kirkuk that were seized during the fight against ISIL, the PUK was divided on the issue. Some PUK members supported Barzani. Other PUK leaders were reluctant to break away from Iraq without a legal resolution to the Kirkuk dispute, which will be discussed in detail in the following chapter, and voiced concern that support for independence from Turkey and Israel would wane. In the midst of the KDP-PUK debate over independence, the Iranian ambas-

---

[47] The Kurdish fighting forces are collectively known as the peshmerga, but the KDP and PUK have control over their own peshmerga units.

[48] Chomani, 2014,

sador to Iraq visited Sulaimaniyah to hold joint talks with the PUK and Gorran.[49] The content of these discussions were not officially made public, but some interpret Iran's actions as an attempt to unite the PUK and Gorran, which would have weakened the KDP's grip over KRG politics at a time when Barzani was pushing for a referendum on independence. In a separate event, the commander of the Quds Brigade, the branch of the Iranian Revolutionary Guard Corps that operates outside Iran, asked the leader of the Gorran Party, Nawshirwan Mustafa, to mediate the internal conflicts in the PUK, thus further demonstrating Iran's willingness to intervene in inter-Kurdish politics.[50] The true extent of Turkey and Iran's interference and influence in the internal Kurdish debate is subject to interpretation, but both nations have a decided interest in whether and how independence occurs.

Conclusions

The Kurdish struggle for independence began nearly 100 years ago, when Western countries introduced the nation-state system to the tribal Middle East. Since then, Kurdish efforts to break away from the Iraqi state have been met with either opposition or indifference from the international community. Abandonment by apparent allies is a pattern in Kurdish history. Moreover, the Kurds have struggled to overcome internal divisions to present a united front in their quest for independence. Prospects for the Kurds' future seemed to improve with the collapse of the Ba'athist regime, but political factions continue to undermine efforts to establish a separate nation. Creating an independent Kurdistan may continue to be an elusive goal unless the Kurdish people are able to overcome the hurdles they have faced in the past.

---

[49] Chomani, 2014.

[50] Hemin Salih, 2015b.

CHAPTER THREE

Iraq's Reaction to an Independent Kurdistan

Iraq's central government has undergone significant changes over the last 12 years as it transitioned from Sunni-led authoritarian rule to an elected government with representatives from Iraq's many ethnic and religious groups. Despite this dramatic change, one policy that has remained consistent is the central government's opposition to Kurdish independence. Since a new government came to power after the collapse of Saddam's regime, there has been nearly constant tension between the KRG and Baghdad over the extent of Kurdish autonomy. From the perspective of the Kurds, who had hoped the end of the Ba'athist era would lead to their independence, any authority Baghdad exerts in the KRG is unwelcome. On the other hand, the central government feels that greater Kurdish autonomy undermines its authority and Iraqi sovereignty. The inherent conflict in these two positions is a strong driver in Erbil-Baghdad relations.

Although the central government opposes further Kurdish autonomy and independence, and despite Baghdad still maintaining some levers of power in the KRG, Baghdad is poorly positioned to prevent the emergence of a Kurdish state. The Iraqi government is paralyzed by sectarian rivalries and undermined by corruption and inefficiency. Major units of the Iraqi Army collapsed in the face of attacks by ISIL, which began seizing towns and villages in Iraq's disputed territories and Sunni provinces in the spring of 2014. The vacuum left by retreating Iraqi Army units enabled the Kurdish peshmerga to seize significant portions of the disputed territories and assume responsibility for defending these areas. Baghdad's ability to fund critical services—

including payments due to the KRG under an established (but often breached) 17 percent revenue sharing formula—is undermined by the drop in global oil prices affecting export revenue obtained by both Baghdad and Erbil.

As noted in Chapter One, in this report we examine three scenarios that could lead to the Kurds gaining independence: a unilateral declaration, independence gained after the disintegration of the Iraqi state, and a gradual and mutual separation. Though Baghdad's current policy toward Kurdish autonomy and independence is well established, our assessment is that the central government would respond differently in each of these scenarios and it is possible its policy with regard to the KRG could evolve over time.

KRG-Baghdad Relations, 2003–Present

The end of the Ba'athist regime ushered in a new era of Iraqi politics. In forming a new post-Saddam government, the United States insisted on creating an inclusive government representative of Iraq's diverse population, presenting Kurds, Shi'a, and many other previously marginalized groups with new opportunities to participate in the political process. For the Kurds, engaging in political decisions in Baghdad enabled them to influence Iraq's policies on Kurdish autonomy. As the TAL and new Iraqi Constitution were crafted in 2004 and 2005, the Kurds used their influence to achieve concessions that limited Baghdad's authority in northern Iraq.[1] Despite the power the Kurds initially wielded in Iraq's new government, Kurdish influence began to wane after the January 2005 elections, relative to what it has been in 2003 and 2004. The Sunni boycott of the new government ended in May 2005, and as the Sunni and Shi'a political parties became more organized, they diluted Kurdish political power. That being said, several Kurdish leaders, such as Nechirvan Barzani, Barham Saleh, Jalal Talabani, and Fuad Masum, have still been influential in national issues.

---

[1] Brennan et al., 2013, p. 147.

Many of the concessions the Kurds won in the constitution have become politically contentious. The central government, which has been controlled by Shi'a political parties since Iraq regained sovereignty in 2004, has used its influence to delay enacting constitutional provisions that would weaken Baghdad's authority in the Kurdistan Region.[2] The inherent conflict between the Kurds' ambition for autonomy and independence and Baghdad's desire to assert its influence in northern Iraq is the foundation of the three major disputes that drive Baghdad-Erbil relations: governance of Iraq's disputed territories, Kurdish rights over oil production in the KRG, and the allocation of national revenues to the KRG. These three disputes and the overarching conflict over the role of the central government in northern Iraq have come to define Erbil-Baghdad relations over the past decade. How these issues are resolved (or not resolved) will determine the degree of conflict, economic viability, and success of an independent Kurdistan.

The Disputed Territories

Iraq's disputed territories, pictured in Figure 3.1, stretch from the Iranian border in the east to the Syrian border in the west and separate the predominantly Kurdish north from the largely Arab central and southern areas of country.

The ethnically mixed populations in these territories contain not only Arabs and Kurds, but also Turkmen, Yazidis, and Chaldeans.[3] Kirkuk governorate is particularly controversial. The last reliable Iraqi census, conducted in 1957, showed Kirkuk city as having a majority Turkmen population, while the province had a 47 percent Kurdish minority.[4] In the decades since that census was conducted, the governorate of Kirkuk has experienced significant demographic shifts stemming from Saddam's Arabization policies, which uprooted thousands of Kurdish families and moved large numbers of Arabs into the Kurdistan Region. After Saddam was toppled, a large influx of Kurds moved back to Kirkuk governorate. (The International Organiza-

---

[2] Brennan et al., 2013, p. 148.

[3] Natali, 2008, pp. 433–443.

[4] Kane, 2011.

Figure 3.1
Post-2003 Iraq and the Disputed Territories

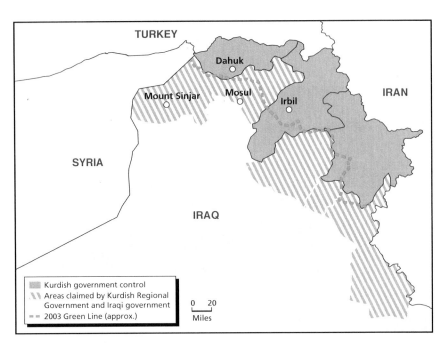

SOURCE: Adapted from Kane, 2011, p. 12.
RAND RR1452-3.1

tion for Migration estimates that more than 20,000 Kurdish families
returned to the governorate between 2003 and the end of 2005 alone.[5])
No accurate assessment of the demographic mix of Kirkuk governorate
currently exists, although a United States Institute for Peace analysis
of 2005 and 2010 national election results suggests that the governorate has only a slight Kurdish majority at most and still has substantial
Turkmen and Arab minority communities.[6]

Control over Kirkuk governorate is contentious because the area
contains vast oil reserves (it is the second-largest oil-producing gov-

---

[5] Cited in Kane, 2011, p. 23.

[6] Kane, 2011, p. 25.

ernorate in Iraq)[7] and because the city of Kirkuk is seen as a historical center of Kurdish society and culture: Jalal Talabani called Kirkuk
the "Kurdish Jerusalem" to highlight how Kurds in Iraq perceive the
city's significance.[8] From Baghdad's perspective, Kurdish administration of Kirkuk and governing over Kirkuk's Arab population (as
well as members of other ethnic groups) would undermine the central government's authority. Furthermore giving the Kurds control over
important oilfields and pipelines would enhance the economic viability
of the Kurdistan Region. Overall, Kurdish control of Kirkuk would
greatly strengthen the Kurds' political and economic arguments for
independence.

Kirkuk's ethnic diversity and fraught history make settling the
dispute over control of this oil-rich province particularly challenging.
Article 140 of the Iraqi Constitution was designed to resolve the conflict
between the KRG and Baghdad over the disputed territories, including
Kirkuk, by mandating the "normalization" of these areas. This process,
which was intended to reverse Saddam's Arabization policies, required
a census to be conducted to determine the demographic make-up on
the disputed territories. The census was to be followed by a referendum
to determine whether these areas would be under the administration of
the KRG.[9] As yet, the measures outlined in the constitution have not
been undertaken, despite UN efforts to lay the groundwork.

Disagreements between Baghdad and Erbil over the disputed territories have driven a wedge between the two governments since Iraq
regained sovereignty. Despite the constitutional provisions setting out
a process to resolve the Kirkuk dispute, given political turmoil in the
region and within Iraq, the central government has avoided taking
steps that could lead to a referendum, which could have resulted in
the KRG gaining control over Kirkuk governorate. Prime Minister
Ibrahim Jaafari, Iraq's first post-Saddam prime minister, rejected Kurd-

[7] Kane, 2011, p. 22.

[8] Quoted in Lake, 2015.

[9] Government of Iraq, 2005.

ish claims to Kirkuk and criticized population movements intended to reverse Saddam's Arabization of Kurdish areas.[10]

Tensions over disputed territories became particularly high during Prime Minister Nouri Maliki's two terms, and several key towns have been flashpoints. After promising to implement Article 140 provisions, Maliki dragged his feet on actually doing so when he first came into office.[11] As Maliki began asserting control over Iraq's security apparatus in 2007 and 2008, he challenged Kurdish power in the disputed territories. In August 2008, a crisis erupted when the Iraqi Security Forces (ISF) entered the Diyala governorate town of Khanaqin, which is near the Iranian border and which the Kurds consider part of historic Kurdistan. By this point in the war, much of the violence caused by the insurgency had been tamped down, and the ISF had proven to be a competent fighting force in certain operations.[12] The peshmerga ignored Baghdad's order to leave Diyala governorate, and an attempt at a brokered settlement failed. The Kurds threatened to engage the Iraqi Army all along the Green Line, the border between KRG-administered Iraq and Baghdad-administered Iraq, and reinforced their positions in Khanaqin. Meanwhile, the central government began moving military assets into Diyala.[13] U.S. intervention ultimately prevented tensions from escalating into armed conflict.

Shortly after the near showdown between ISF and peshmerga in Khanaqin, Maliki attempted to supplant Kurdish influence in Kirkuk. In November 2008, Maliki tried to organize groups that could challenge the Kurds and announced the establishment of councils in the disputed territories composed of Arabs, Turkmens, and Kurds opposed to KDP and PUK's leadership.[14] Maliki reached out to Kirkuk's Arab tribes, and soon thereafter demonstrations proclaiming Arab ties to Kirkuk province broke out.

---

[10] Allawi, 2008, p. 410.

[11] Kutschera, 2007, pp. 10–12.

[12] Gordon and Trainor, 2012, p. 545.

[13] Gordon and Trainor, 2012, p. 547.

[14] Stansfield and Anderson, 2009, pp. 134–145.

Political conflicts over authority in the disputed territories have emerged in more recent years. In 2012, Maliki again attempted to assert Baghdad's control in the disputed territories by announcing the creation of the Dijla Operations Command, which put the provinces of Kirkuk, Diyala, and Salah al-Din under the purview of the ISF.[15] The Kurds felt threatened by Maliki's military buildup, leading to a stand-off between the ISF and peshmerga forces.[16] Tensions heightened again in the late spring and summer of 2014, after the peshmerga seized large sections of the disputed territories, including the city of Kirkuk, during the ISIL invasion of Iraq. Soon thereafter, Barzani called for a referendum on independence to be held in the Kurdistan Region.[17] Maliki rejected the KRG's claim that it would retain control of the area and accused the Kurds of exploiting the instability caused by ISIL.[18] After Maliki accused the Kurds of allowing ISIL fighters and former Ba'athist members to use Erbil as a base of operations, the Kurdish political bloc withdrew its participation in the central government until the prime minister apologized.[19] A month after the peshmerga first entered Kirkuk and seized its surrounding oilfields, Kurds forced Arab workers out of the Kirkuk and Bai Hassan oilfields, a move that Baghdad's ministry of oil called "a violation of the Constitution and national wealth."[20]

Shortly after the Kurds seized Kirkuk, Haider Abadi replaced Maliki as prime minister. Since then, the political discourse surrounding control of Kirkuk and other disputed territories has been much less heated. Despite the cooling of tensions and the ability of Baghdad and Erbil to reach compromises on other contentious issues, the two governments have still not reconciled their differences over control of

---

[15] Sullivan, 2013.

[16] "Iraqi Kurds Send More Troops into Standoff with Iraq Army," 2012.

[17] Salman and Mahmoud, 2014.

[18] "Al-Maliki Rules Out Poll on Kurdish Independence," 2014.

[19] Salman and Mahmoud, 2014; "Al-Maliki Rules Out Poll on Kurdish Independence," 2014.

[20] Quoted in "Kurdish Troops Seize Iraq's Kirkuk, Bai Hassan Oilfields," 2014.

the disputed territories. Like Maliki and Jaafari, Abadi has not fulfilled constitutional requirements regarding Kirkuk. The referendum in the disputed territories called for in Article 140 has not been held, and although Kirkuk is currently under Kurdish control, the legal status of the province remains unresolved.

The KRG gaining control over Kirkuk and its surrounding oil-fields in 2014 was a major victory from the perspective of Iraq's Kurds. For Baghdad, losing control over Kirkuk and its oil was an embarrassment and revealed the Iraqi Army's inability to defend the country from the onslaught of ISIL. The central government protests the continuing Kurdish administration of Kirkuk. It is unlikely to abandon its claims over the oil-rich province, as well as other disputed territories seized by the KRG in 2014. If the KRG separates from Iraq, how the control over Kirkuk is resolved will be crucial in determining whether Kurdish independence leads to conflict with Baghdad.

Disagreements Regarding the Kurdish Oil Industry

Both the KRG and Baghdad see the unilateral development of the Kurdish oil industry as furthering Kurdish autonomy by making the Kurdistan Region financially self-sustaining, which is why disputes over ownership and rights to produce and export oil are difficult to resolve. The constitution is ambiguous about the role of regional governments in oil and gas development. Article 112 states, "The federal government, with the producing governorates and regional governments, shall undertake the management of oil and gas extracted from present fields. . . ."[21] From the Kurds' perspective, this article denies the central government the right to manage oil produced from reserves newly discovered after the ratification of the constitution, most of which have been in areas under control of the KRG.[22] Baghdad believes this provision gives it oversight authority over all Iraqi oil production and that any oil exports from Kurdish territories not controlled by SOMO are illegal.[23]

---

[21] Government of Iraq, 2005.

[22] Voller, 2013, p. 72.

[23] Van Heuvelen and Lando, 2014.

Efforts to pass a national oil and gas law that clarifies the ambiguity over the rights of provinces to independently develop their oil resources have been unsuccessful, and in 2007 the Kurds adopted an oil and gas law in their regional parliament that provides for exploitation of natural resources in their territory.[24] Shortly after the passage of this law, the KRG announced it would offer blocks to international oil companies under production-sharing contracts.[25] Kurdish oilfields began attracting small- and medium-sized oil companies. But by 2012, the KRG also had signed exploration contracts with major international oil companies (IOCs), such as ExxonMobil, Gazprom Neft, Total, and Chevron.[26]

Despite some success in attracting oil investors, which have found and developed commercial fields, the KRG now faces significant challenges to transporting oil out of the Kurdistan Region. Production capacity in the KRG, including areas seized in the disputed territories in June 2014, averaged 612,367 barrels per day (bpd) in 2015.[27] The KRG pipeline and the DNO/Tawke pipeline—two main pipelines the KRG relies on for moving oil across the border with Turkey, where the oil then flows into the existing Iraq-Turkey pipeline—have a combined capacity to export 400,000 bpd.[28] The KRG also uses trucks to transport between 50,000 and 100,000 bpd by road to export hubs in Turkey and Iran. At the end of 2014, combined pipeline and trucking export infrastructure fell short of production capacity. Plans to expand export capacity have been announced but have not yet been completed.

To hinder Kurdish efforts to develop its oil industry, the central government has implemented a strategy to obstruct unilateral oil development by punishing actors in the oil industry that facilitate Kurdish exports. Once the Kurds began to pursue oil contracts unilaterally,

---

[24] Kurdistan Regional Government, 2007.

[25] Voller, 2013, p. 72.

[26] Hiltermann, 2012.

[27] Kurdistan Regional Government, Ministry of Natural Resources, 2016.

[28] U.S. Energy Information Administration, undated.

Baghdad maintained that the production-sharing contracts[29] the KRG signed with IOCs were unconstitutional and lacked transparency and accused the KRG of corruption in not declaring signing bonus revenue.[30] In 2008, Iraq's oil minister declared international oil company contracts with the KRG to be "illegal and illegitimate" and threatened to revoke Baghdad's contracts with companies that also had signed contracts with the KRG.[31] In effect, this step would have required oil companies to choose between the central government's larger and well-established oil sector and the smaller, faster-growing oil sector in the Kurdistan Region. In November 2011, the KRG announced that, notwithstanding the central government's objections, an agreement had been reached with ExxonMobil, which included authorization to explore potential oilfields in a disputed part of Kirkuk.[32] Baghdad's response was even stronger than previous reactions to unilateral Kurdish oil contracts. Not only did Baghdad announce that ExxonMobil would be excluded from the next round of bidding for oil rights,[33] but the central government began to bar companies indirectly involved in the KRG's oil industry from obtaining contracts for oil development elsewhere in Iraq.[34] However, much of this appears to be bluff. ExxonMobil still continues to manage the West Qurna field in southern Iraq under a technical service contract with Baghdad's Ministry of Oil.

In addition to punishing oil companies that signed contracts with the KRG, Baghdad has also brought legal action against several parties involved in purchasing Kurdish oil as part of its effort to keep the oil exports from the Kurdistan Region under the central government's control. The central government maintains that the constitution and Iraqi law bans exporting Kurdish oil through companies other than

---

[29] Production-sharing contracts are contracts between a government and an oil company that stipulates how much of the revenue from oil sales the government will receive.

[30] Zulal, 2011.

[31] Quoted in Voller, 2013, p. 73.

[32] Voller, 2013, p. 73.

[33] Trompiz and Driver, 2012.

[34] Voller, 2013, p. 73.

SOMO, and therefore Baghdad has brought legal action against the pipeline, port, shippers, and buyers of Kurdish crude. In May 2014, the KRG nonetheless unilaterally began exporting oil through pipelines to Turkey despite Baghdad's objections, and in response the central government took legal action against the Turkish government and the Turkish pipeline company, Botas, in an international court for their involvement in Kurdish exports.[35] Baghdad also threatened to take legal action against the port inspectors at Ceyhan for allowing Kurdish oil to be exported. In July 2014, Iraq took legal action in U.S. courts to prevent the *United Kalavyrta*, a vessel carrying 1 million barrels of Kurdish oil, from offloading its cargo in Texas.[36] In September 2014, Baghdad announced that it was suing Marine Management Services, the owner of the first vessel to load Kurdish oil, for $318 million in retaliation for what Baghdad claims is the illegal export of Iraqi crude.[37]

Although unilateral Kurdish oil exports have continued, this series of legal challenges was successful in undermining the reputation the Kurds hoped to establish as a reliable oil exporter. Indeed, Kurdish-origin oil is in many ways a gray-market good. Most buyers demand secrecy when buying Kurdish crude, leading the KRG to go to great lengths to disguise oil purchases. For example, countries often bar ships from offloading Kurdish crude in their ports to avoid legal ramifications. Consequently, vessels transporting Kurdish crude frequently transfer the oil to another ship while at sea to disguise the origin of the cargo, thereby protecting buyers from potential legal action by Baghdad.[38] The Kurds also are forced to sell oil well below market value.[39] As long as oil prices remain low in the near and medium term and the Kurds lack the export infrastructure and legitimacy as an oil producer, the KRG will struggle to become financially self-sustaining.

---

[35] Pirog, 2014.

[36] Van Heuvelen, Lando, and Osgood, 2015.

[37] Pirog, 2014, p. 3.

[38] Van Heuvelen, Lando, and Osgood, 2015.

[39] Natali et al., 2015.

Budget Disputes

Another related ongoing dispute between the KRG and central government is over the sharing of national revenues. According to Article 121 of the Iraqi Constitution, "Regions and governorates shall be allocated an equitable share of the national revenues sufficient to discharge their responsibilities and duties, but having regard to their resources, needs, and the percentage of their population."[40] Baghdad and Erbil representatives agreed in 2004 that Baghdad would transfer to Erbil 17 percent of net federal revenues, but Baghdad and Erbil disagree on exactly which expenses this allocation should cover.[41] Like the constitutional provisions addressing oil production and management, the ambiguities of the constitution and the different interpretations of what the central government is required to provide the KRG have led to disagreements between Erbil and Baghdad.

One conflict relates to Iraq's support for the peshmerga, the Kurdish security forces. Baghdad is reluctant to provide financial support to Kurdish fighters, because the strength of this force diminishes the KRG's reliance on Baghdad for security. The central government has argued that expenses related to maintaining the peshmerga should be covered by the 17 percent of the federal budget provided to the KRG.[42] Baghdad's basis for this argument stems from Article 121 of the constitution, which states, "the regional government shall be responsible for all the administrative requirements of the region, particularly the establishment and organization of the internal security forces. . . ."[43] The Kurds believe that a different constitutional provision requires Baghdad to pay for the peshmerga, as they are part of Iraq's armed forces and are charged with defending the country.[44] After the 2007 budget law seemed to resolve this dispute, with Baghdad now being required to pay for peshmerga expenses, another dispute arose over the

---

[40] Government of Iraq, 2005.

[41] Brennan et al., 2013, p. 150.

[42] Brennan et al., 2013, p. 150.

[43] Government of Iraq, 2005.

[44] Brennan et al., 2013, p. 150.

size of the peshmerga force.[45] The KRG argued the budget law required Baghdad to pay the salaries for 100,000 active duty peshmerga as well as the pensions of 90,000 peshmerga veterans. The central government, on the other hand, maintained that the peshmerga force should include only 30,000 troops and that payments to the militia's veterans should be the regional government's responsibility. In 2010, the Maliki administration agreed to contribute funds to a peshmerga force of 100,000 soldiers, provided that 30,000 of them are integrated into the Iraqi Army. While this seemed to resolve the budget issue over the peshmerga, Erbil has not consistently received the funding the federal government agreed to provide.

Another budget dispute that has not been resolved is the total amount the central government owes the KRG on a monthly basis. As noted, Baghdad argues that sovereign expenses should be deducted from the budget and the Kurds should be allocated 17 percent of the remaining funds, which is approximately 10 percent to 13 percent of the initial government budget.[46] The KRG argues that its own administrative costs should be paid for by the central government in addition to the monthly budget payment it receives. The KRG argues that either (1) Baghdad should pay for the KRG's sovereign costs as part of Iraq's sovereign costs and provide the Kurds the remaining 17 percent of the budget or (2) the KRG should be given 17 percent of the initial budget before sovereign costs are deducted, thus providing the KRG the funding needed to support its administration.[47]

The KRG was heavily reliant on payments from Baghdad, which prior to 2015 accounted for 95 percent of the KRG's budget.[48] Salaries alone represent a monthly burden of $670 million.[49] Between the KRG's 682,000 civil servants and the 718,000 people receiving government pensions, the Kurdish government is responsible for provid-

[45] Brennan et al., 2013, p. 150.

[46] Van Heuvelen and Lando, 2014.

[47] Van Heuvelen and Lando, 2014.

[48] Natali, 2008, p. 436.

[49] Knights, 2014.

ing monthly payments to one in every three inhabitants in the Kurd-istan Region.[50] Without monthly payments from Baghdad, the KRG cannot make its payroll commitments. The central government uses Erbil's financial dependence to influence the KRG, and in recent years the budget dispute has become intertwined with disagreements over Kurdish oil production. In early 2014, Prime Minister Maliki halted monthly payments after accusing the KRG of not delivering the agreed amount of oil to SOMO.[51] The decision was devastating to the KRG. Erbil was forced to approach buyers to request advance payments for oil exports and loans.[52] The KRG could not afford to repay the loans when they fell due in the fall of 2014, and subsequently stopped paying its obligations to IOCs operating producing wells in the Kurdistan Region. The KRG's debt level rose rapidly, and IOCs began paring back their rate of exploration and production investment.

The Kurds' economic situation and the change of prime min-ister in Baghdad from Maliki to Haider Abadi helped set the stage for constructive negotiations between Baghdad and Erbil in late 2014 covering revenue sharing and Kurdish oil production and exports in the context of the Kurdistan Region's then-recent assumption of con-trol over the Kirkuk fields. In November 2014, the KRG agreed to provide 150,000 bpd to SOMO in exchange for a one-time payment of $500 million, to ease the short-term financial pressure on Erbil.[53] This agreement paved the way for a follow-on deal that envisaged that the Kurds would provide 250,000 bpd of their region's oil pro-duction to SOMO for sale in international markets and facilitate the export of 300,000 bpd from Kirkuk's oilfields. This would have been in exchange for transfers of $12 billion in 2015, which would have rep-resented approximately 17 percent of Iraq's anticipated federal revenues for the year.[54]

---

[50] Osgood and Tahir, 2015.

[51] Knights, 2014.

[52] Osgood, 2015.

[53] Smith and staff, 2015.

[54] Smith and staff, 2015.

Though an agreement was reached and relations between the KRG and Baghdad have improved since Abadi became prime minister, both parties feel the other has not fully satisfied its obligations under this agreement. Baghdad soon claimed the Kurds had not provided the volume of oil agreed upon, and Erbil insisted that Baghdad had failed to make the agreed regular payments to the KRG. Disputes remain over whether the Kurds can unilaterally export oil, and some members of the Iraqi parliament attempted to amend the 2015 budget to include language prohibiting Kurdish exports beyond what is required to supply to SOMO.[55] Meanwhile, the KRG's minister for natural resources called the right to export a "red line."[56] So, despite the apparent progress made in late 2014, disagreements over the implementation of the budget agreement persist.

Baghdad's Response to Kurdish Independence

Iraq's central government and its policies have changed dramatically since the overthrow of Saddam's regime, but Baghdad's in-principle opposition to Kurdish independence has not wavered. The central government continues to see the potential breakaway of the Kurdistan Region as incompatible with Iraqi sovereignty, particularly if the new Kurdish state includes portions of the disputed territories that contain oil. However, the situation in Iraq could evolve in such a way that the central government's opposition to Kurdish independence wanes. This weakened opposition could be the result of (1) Baghdad determining that it has more to benefit from Kurdish independence than it does from preventing Kurdish secession or (2) Kurdish independence seeming inevitable, leading Baghdad to enter into separation negotiations for a lack of other options. The central government's reaction to the establishment of an independent Kurdistan and the tools Baghdad has available to either undermine or facilitate Kurdish sovereignty would vary depending on how independence is achieved.

---

[55] Tahir and Osgood, 2015.

[56] Tahir and Osgood, 2015.

The discussion below outlines different ways in which the Kurds could gain independence and how Baghdad is likely to respond in each scenario. The conclusions drawn in this section are based on the analysis presented above and projections based on Baghdad's past behavior and the realities of other issues the central government currently faces or could face in the future.

Unilateral Declaration of Kurdish Independence

In this scenario, the KRG unilaterally declares independence from Iraq—perhaps abruptly, or perhaps following a successful referendum on independence over the objections of the central government. Of all the scenarios that will be explored here, Kurdish independence gained in this manner is likely to provoke the most hostile response from Baghdad, particularly if the KRG asserts that the governorate of Kirkuk and non-Kurdish territory liberated from ISIL would be part of the new state. The central government could see this unilateral action as an affront to Iraqi sovereignty and as a serious challenge to Baghdad's ability to keep the rest of the country united. Consequently, Baghdad is likely to react strongly. Baghdad could use different measures within its grasp to punish the Kurds for resisting the central government's authority, make independence as painful and unsuccessful as possible, undermine the economic viability of the new state, and alter the Kurds' cost-benefit analysis of independence.

One of the first steps Baghdad could take in this scenario would be to end any possibility of monthly revenue-sharing payments under the guise of the 2004 17 percent arrangement. The impact of this action could be significant, as demonstrated by the financial woes the KRG has experienced since early 2014, when Maliki suspended budget payments, and subsequently since the collapse of the late 2014 budget deal involving commercialization of the Kirkuk area oil. Without revenue sharing, the KRG has been unable to meet its financial obligations; consequently, oil companies have become more reluctant to invest in the Kurdistan Region, and those already there have scaled back their activities.[57] Unless the KRG becomes more financially sus-

---

[57] Osgood, 2015.

tainable before declaring independence, the central government's cessation of even the possibility of monthly payments could aggravate such effects. Baghdad could exacerbate the impact of this financial crunch if it also stopped financially supporting the peshmerga. This would force the KRG to support more peshmerga fighters and to fully fund its own defense, which would be more costly once the KRG became solely responsible for security along the border it shares with ISIL.

In some ways, the situation as of mid-2015 was a practice run for what happens to the KRG when forced to support the peshmerga and do without financial assistance from Baghdad. Baghdad's payments to the KRG have been sporadic and lower than expected throughout 2015. This included payments for the peshmerga. As a result, the KRG was, in effect, solely responsible for security along its ISIL border, although there were reports of assistance from PKK fighters, Shi'a militias as part of the Popular Mobilization Units, and even ISF. Furthermore, the KRG experienced a significant economic crisis in 2015 as a result of Baghdad not delivering budget payments. While facing a budget deficit, low global oil prices, and ongoing operations against ISIL, the Kurdistan Parliament passed a bill allowing the KRG to borrow up to $5 billion from private banks.[58] This move reveals how fragile the Kurdish economy is. Given this reality, an independent Kurdistan that relies on outside actors for financial stability may not be economically viable.

Baghdad could further punish the Kurds by blocking access to southern Iraq, thus forcing the KRG to rely on Turkey and Iran for all import and export activity. In practice, the KRG is already dependent on Turkey and Iran for export routes, but announcing that no Kurdish or foreign goods could cross Kurdistan's new southern border would highlight this economic reliance. The symbolism of this reliance could undermine the new state's legitimacy. Moreover, this would affect Kurdish companies that have investments in southern and central Iraq, such as Asiacell and Korek, two of the KRG's most successful corporations.[59] Kurdish trading companies import from Turkey

---

[58] Mohammad Salih, 2015b.

[59] Invest in Group, 2013, p. 134.

and Iran for resale to other Iraqi regions. Although Iraqi companies in southern and central Iraq with investments in the Kurdistan Region would also suffer from this blockade, denying the Kurds access to the rest of Iraq would serve Baghdad's purpose of highlighting the KRG's economic weaknesses.

Additionally, the central government could create social and political havoc in the Kurdistan Region by expelling Kurds that live outside the boundaries of the new state. Forcing the Kurdish segment of the Iraqi population to seek refuge in the Kurdistan Region could aggravate an already significant humanitarian crisis. Given that the KRG currently hosts hundreds of thousands of refugees and well over 1 million IDPs who have fled ISIL and the Syrian civil war, being forced to allow Kurds from all over Iraq into the Kurdistan Region would add further social and economic pressure to the newly independent nation. However, foreseeing the impact of this action is difficult. Before the war, approximately 1 million Kurds lived in Baghdad, but Iraq's significant population shifts since 2003 and failure to conduct a national census make it difficult to know exactly how many Kurds currently live outside the KRG and disputed territories.[60] If most of Iraq's Kurds have already relocated to the Kurdistan Region or are living in the disputed territories, which the KRG largely controls, the impact of Baghdad's expulsion may be limited; if there is still a sizable Kurdish population living in Baghdad and elsewhere in Iraq, forcing these people from their homes could create a significant problem for the KRG.

Militarily, Baghdad's options are limited in this scenario. ISIL's ascent revealed the weakness of the Iraqi military, and today Baghdad must rely on U.S. air strikes and support from Iranian-backed Shi'a militias to push the insurgents back across the Syrian border. While Baghdad could divert resources from its fight against ISIL to open a front against the Kurds, it may be difficult for Baghdad to devote enough resources to succeed, given Iraq's many security priorities. This may continue to be true even after the Iraqi Army is no longer engaged with ISIL. Furthermore, Baghdad may not be able to rely on military support from other nations—particularly Turkey and Iran—to oppose

---

[60] Safire, 2003.

Kurdish independence with force. As will be discussed in later chapters, Turkey and Iran, two countries that would be greatly affected by Kurdish independence, may not oppose the emergence of a Kurdish state.

The international community's reaction to Kurdish independence gained in this manner could also provide Baghdad with options for opposing the KRG's actions. Other countries could see unilaterally declaring independence as a rash, irresponsible decision that creates further instability in an already tumultuous region. The Kurds are unlikely to gain the support of the international community if their actions are seen as exacerbating the Middle East's security problems, particularly if independence was thought to compromise the fight against ISIL. Furthermore, Prime Minister Abadi has shown a greater willingness to work with the Kurds than his predecessor, Nouri Maliki. If Abadi continued cooperation with the KRG prior to the unilateral declaration of independence examined in this scenario, the Kurds would be less able to claim that Baghdad's authoritarianism justified breaking away from Iraq. This could make gaining the support of the international community even more difficult. Baghdad could leverage the international community's uncertainty about independence under these conditions by positioning itself as the innocent victim of instability caused by Kurdistan's perceived unwarranted secession. This would undermine the KRG's ability to establish legitimacy as an independent nation.

Nevertheless, we assume that Baghdad's response in this scenario would be strong. Though the central government may lack a viable military option, the high toll its other actions would exact on the Kurds could sufficiently affect the KRG's cost-benefit analysis of unilaterally declaring independence. Indeed, in 2014, when Baghdad's disarray made Kurdish independence seem likely, the Kurds backed off the idea of holding a referendum. Compared with the chaos that gripped Baghdad as ISIL advanced from newly conquered Mosul through the western part of Iraq, the KRG looked relatively capable and effective, even though U.S. assistance was required to repel ISIL. Despite the Kurds claiming self-sufficiency, the KRG in the end did not hold a referendum on independence. Moreover, the economic crisis the KRG faced in the summer of 2015 demonstrated that the KRG may not be economically viable without assistance from an outside actor, which a Kurdistan created through a unilateral declaration might lack. It seems that the downsides of a unilateral declaration of independence have been too great in recent years, suggesting that it is less likely that the Kurds would benefit by seeking independence in this manner going forward.

Last Man Standing

In the previous scenario, Baghdad would likely oppose Kurdish independence because it makes the central government appear weak; in this scenario, Kurdish independence is the direct result of the central government's aggravated weakness. If Iraqi central authorities should collapse through the secession of Basra, Baghdad succumbing to ISIL's control, a military coup, or other possible ways, and if the central government were no longer able to provide services or function at a basic level, Baghdad would have very few options available to punish the Kurds and alter Erbil's cost-benefit analysis of independence. Though Baghdad is largely powerless in this scenario, the Kurds could experience many of the same pressures as in the previous scenario; however, the result of these burdens on Kurdish independence could be very different.

Many of the potential sources of leverage Baghdad possessed in the previous scenario would no longer exist if the Iraqi state disintegrated. Assuming that payments from Baghdad to Erbil have resumed, which as of spring 2016 they have not, the central government would once again stop providing the KRG monthly payments, not because it wants to punish or manipulate the Kurds, but because Baghdad is no longer capable of collecting and disseminating revenue. The Kurds could use this to justify their decision to separate from Iraq. The economic impact on the Kurds of losing their share of federal revenues would be similar to what was described previously, but the origin of this economic pressure would be Baghdad's failure to maintain a functioning government rather than a Kurdish unilateral decision to declare independence.

Furthermore, Baghdad would not intentionally be able to isolate the Kurds from southern and central Iraq as a punishment for independence. If the Iraqi state collapsed, the ensuing chaos would likely isolate the Kurds from the rest of Iraq anyway, thus preventing Baghdad from purposefully using its own leverage to prevent or punish Kurdish independence. That same chaos also could create the refugee crisis described in the previous scenario. If Baghdad were no longer able to provide basic services, Arab Iraqis living under the central government's authority in Baghdad and the south also could seek to move to Kurdish areas. The Kurds would have to choose between shouldering the social and economic burdens of supporting more refugees (with likely international help) or further fortifying the border to keep them out (which would affect their international standing). While in the previous scenario any refugee crisis and increased pressure on the peshmerga stemmed from intentional actions by Baghdad, in this case they would be the consequences of the central government's collapse.

Militarily, in the last-man-standing scenario, Baghdad could have even fewer options. Iraq's military is still recovering and regrouping from ISIL's 2014 onslaught, and the state's collapse could undermine any progress made in reconstituting an effective army. Baghdad may be likely to use its limited military resources to seek to regain or retain control of areas within its grasp, if it is even capable of doing so. The probability of Baghdad having any resources available to challenge the Kurds is low, and the odds that a military effort against the KRG would succeed are slim.

In this scenario, the international community could be more understanding of Kurdish independence, thus depriving Baghdad of the ability to leverage international opposition against the Kurds. Kurdish independence in this case could be seen as a consequence of Baghdad's collapse, not the result of the KRG overstepping its bounds. The international community is unlikely to actively oppose Kurdish independence and could tacitly, or even explicitly, support the effort to establish an independent state. Given the economic troubles an independent Kurdistan would face without revenue-sharing payments from Baghdad, this support would be crucial in making the new nation more economically sound. As seen in 2014 and 2015, the KRG is not economically viable without substantial oil-related revenue; however, a Kurdistan that has legitimacy may be able to further develop its oil industry and realize full world oil prices without discounts on the global market. If Kurdistan were able to compensate for the lost financial support it once received from Baghdad with investment from the international community, the chances that Kurdistan succeeds as an independent country improve.

The consequences of Baghdad's actions in the first scenario are similar to the impact that Iraq's collapse could have on the KRG, but the overall outcome regarding Kurdish independence is drastically different. In this scenario, the Kurds pursue independence because remaining in the Iraqi state is no longer viable. Baghdad would have few options for punishing the Kurds for breaking away completely. As a result, Baghdad would be unable to alter the KRG's cost-benefit analysis regarding the consequences of independence, and the Kurds could better achieve their goal without shouldering the responsibility for breaking up Iraq. Rather than being accused of causing greater chaos in the Middle East, the Kurds could be seen as the only remaining semblance of stability in a volatile region.

Gradual Estrangement

Unlike the scenarios in which Baghdad has no control over Kurdish efforts to gain independence, the central government plays a role in how independence is achieved in the event of a gradual estrangement between Baghdad and Erbil. In this scenario, years of stalled negotiations over contentious disputes could lead to several possible outcomes. One is that Baghdad could willingly enter into negotiations to allow the KRG to secede, after concluding that separation with the Kurds is the best way forward for Iraq. In this case, the evolution of Kurdish-Baghdad relations has altered the central government's calculus to such an extent that an amicable secession is perceived as more beneficial than maintaining the status quo. For example, if Baghdad's strategy to prevent Kurdish oil expansion failed, the Kurds gained legitimacy as an oil exporter, and the disputes over sharing oil revenues remained unresolved, the central government could decide that a negotiated separation may be in its best interests. In this instance, the central government could be willing to grant the KRG independence in exchange for sharing the revenues from the oilfields in the disputed territories, particularly Kirkuk's oilfields.

Alternatively, if Baghdad no longer had any way to prevent Kurdish independence, the need to mitigate the consequences of the emergence of a Kurdish state could force Baghdad into negotiations it otherwise would oppose. This could happen if the KRG developed a prosperous oil industry that made the Kurdistan Region financially independent of Baghdad and if the peshmerga forces were to improve their capabilities to such an extent that the KRG could provide for all its security needs without outside assistance, including defending the border with ISIL. If this situation emerged in northern Iraq, Baghdad would be unable to use financial or military leverage to prevent Kurdish secession and might be willing to negotiate a separation that mitigated the impact on Baghdad.

Regardless of the exact circumstances in which a gradual estrangement occurs, there are several things Baghdad could do to facilitate an amicable separation. First, although the central government would be unlikely to continue revenue-sharing payments to the KRG after the Kurds gained independence, rather than cutting off payments in an attempt to exploit the KRG's dependence on Baghdad, the central government could slowly reduce payments in a manner that enabled the KRG to incrementally take on more financial responsibilities. In this way, Baghdad could help the KRG become financially sustainable.

In a negotiated separation, Baghdad and Erbil would need to address territorial disputes. As previously mentioned, the KRG seized about 90 percent of the disputed territories in 2014. For a separation between Iraq and Kurdistan to succeed without creating the possibility of future conflict, clearly delineated borders would need to be established between these two countries. To achieve this, Erbil may need to be willing to return some parts of the disputed territories it currently occupies. Given the historic tensions between Baghdad and Erbil over the disputed territories and the ethnically mixed population that resides in this region, a deliberate and mediated process to establish a new border between Iraq and Kurdistan is necessary to avoid the creation of potential future flashpoints between these neighboring countries.

Furthermore, a gradual estrangement followed by a negotiated settlement would need to address disagreements over oil production. To facilitate this process, Baghdad could agree to drop its claims of ownership over oil in the KRG's three original provinces in exchange for oil revenue from the disputed territories that would now be part of Kurdistan. As noted previously, the central government's opposition to unilateral Kurdish oil exports, even from production in the KRG's three original provinces, has undermined the development of the Kurdish oil industry. As part of a negotiated settlement, Baghdad could exchange Kurdish independence, and with that control over the KRG's oil industry, for a share of the profits from oil production in the disputed territories that are incorporated into the new Kurdish state or managed jointly, as a small oilfield is on the Iraqi-Kuwaiti border. This would help resolve disagreements over the disputed territories, particularly the oil-rich province of Kirkuk, and facilitate the swift development of the oil sector in both the territory originally incorporated into the KRG and the formerly disputed territories. Both Baghdad and Erbil would benefit from this arrangement. Baghdad would receive a portion of the revenue from Kirkuki oil, while Kurdistan would finally be able to maximize profits from production in all its oilfields. An agreement like this could help break the stalemate over the disputed territories and enable an independent Kurdistan and the rest of Iraq to move toward a mutually beneficial relationship.

An agreement that resolves issues over the disputed territories and their oilfields would also need to address population transfers between Iraq and Kurdistan. Depending on division of the land, parts of the now-disputed territories that would become part of an independent Kurdistan are now ethnically mixed. Kurdistan and Iraq would need to come to an agreement that allowed Arabs in Kurdish territory to return to Iraq and Kurds in Iraq to return to Kurdistan. Furthermore, the non-Kurdish and non-Arab populations, such as the Turkmen, should be free to choose in which nation they live, and be assured a right to stay in their homes if they wished to do so. Additionally, both Iraq and Kurdistan would need to ensure that their respective minority populations that choose to stay are granted the same rights as the majority. Guaranteeing that all those moving are treated humanely and welcomed into their new country would minimize the negative consequences of a population transfer and reduce the risk that animosity develops between these neighboring countries.

Baghdad also could ease the return of peshmerga forces that had been integrated into the Iraqi Army that would be transferred back to the regular peshmerga. An amicable agreement on the separation of Kurdish troops—one that addresses ownership of equipment, payment of salaries, pensions, and other matters—could pave the way for future constructive military-to-military relations between the Iraqi Army and the army of Kurdistan. A phased separation, for example, could minimize the financial burden to the KRG of integrating these troops into the regular Kurdish security forces, while enabling the Iraqi Army to deploy them against ISIL in the interim. Given that Iraq and an independent Kurdistan would face several mutual threats, such as sharing borders with ISIL and the humanitarian challenges stemming from the Syrian civil war, military cooperation would greatly enhance the security of both.

The gradual estrangement and ensuing negotiated separation of Baghdad and Erbil would most likely facilitate the emergence of a sovereign Kurdish state. Such a dynamic would minimize the extent to which Baghdad raises objections to Kurdish secession, and the international community is less likely to oppose Kurdish independence if Baghdad agrees to it. A peaceful divorce would thus leave Erbil well positioned to launch a newly independent Kurdish state.

The Influence of Kurdish Nationalism

All three scenarios—a unilateral declaration of independence, last man standing, and gradual estrangement—could coincide with the emergence of a pan-Kurdish movement inspired by the Iraqi Kurds' successes. Though the Kurds in Iraq, Iran, Turkey, and Syria are politically divided, it is conceivable that, with independence at some point in the future, Iraqi Kurdish leader Masoud Barzani could grow in political significance in relation to other Kurdish leaders in adjacent countries. The prospects for successful Kurdish secession could be jeopardized if

Barzani, whether intentionally or not, inspired a resurgence of Kurdish nationalism among Kurds in Iran, Syria, and Turkey. Though the pan-Kurdish effect is itself not a separate scenario in our analysis, this is an important dynamic that could significantly influence how the emergence of a Kurdish state is perceived in the region.

Of all countries with an interest in Kurdish independence, Turkey and Iran are the most likely to feel threatened by a resurgence of pan-Kurdish nationalism. Turkey has spent nearly a decade attempting to integrate its Kurdish population into Turkish society, but this may have reached a potentially temporary stop with renewed Turkey-PKK violence in August 2015. Meanwhile, Iran has worked to stifle Kurdish nationalism within its borders. If Ankara, Tehran, and Baghdad all believed that a sovereign Kurdish state would be an irredentist challenge to their own domestic stability, all three of the Kurdistan Region's neighbors could work together to undermine Erbil's claim to statehood.

Baghdad's options for a unilateral military response in the two scenarios in which it cannot prevent Kurdish independence are limited. However, if the emergence of a pan-Kurdish appeal threatened Ankara or Tehran's efforts to control their domestic Kurdish populations, Baghdad could have an opportunity to enhance its military cooperation with either Turkey or Iran. This could enable the central government to challenge the threat it perceives from Kurdish independence without overextending Baghdad's military. However, the attraction of Baghdad as a military partner could be diminished in the scenario in which Iraq collapses. Other nations may be more reluctant to offer military assistance, especially lethal military aid, to a government that has limited resources or may be unable to control the aid provided.

Baghdad could also seek cooperation on the economic punishment it exacts on the KRG. For example, if Turkey were to fear that Kurdish independence would generate domestic instability, Baghdad and Ankara could work together to isolate northern Iraq economically. Without access to Turkey's oil export infrastructure, the Kurds would need to rely on exports through southern Iraq or by truck through Iran or even Syria. However, trucks on these routes cannot carry enough oil to sustain Kurdistan independence, and if the southern route were also blocked, very little Kurdish oil could be exported, which could be economically disastrous for the Kurds.

Iran and Turkey could also assist in the social and political havoc Baghdad could create to punish the Kurds for gaining independence. If Iran or Turkey were to close the borders after Baghdad expelled Kurds from non-Kurdish areas, the KRG would be forced to shoulder the full burden of the flood of refugees. Closing the border could also intensify the economic strain on the KRG by stifling export-based economic activity. The economic and political pressure this could create for the KDP and PUK would be tremendous.

Given the potential ramifications of Iraq collaborating with Turkey or Iran to undermine independence, it would benefit the Kurds to tamp down pan-Kurdish nationalism leading up to independence in the unilateral declaration and last-man-standing scenarios. However, if pan-Kurdish appeal accompanied independence in the gradual estrangement scenario, Baghdad would likely respond to Turkey and Iran's potential opposition to Kurdish independence differently, as a negotiated settlement benefits Baghdad in this situation. Rather than coordinate efforts to undermine the KRG, Baghdad could work with the Kurds to mitigate the effects of any Iranian or Turkish backlash. For example, Baghdad could facilitate oil transport through southern Iraq if Turkey blocked Kurdish oil exports (though this would require the completion of a functioning north-south crude pipeline link, at considerable cost). This action could help the Kurds retain their financial viability in the face of Turkish hostility while deepening economic relations with Baghdad. This is just one way in which Baghdad could alleviate the impact of Turkish or Iranian hostility toward the new nation.

Conclusion

Iraq's central government has opposed Kurdish autonomy and independence for years, leading to significant political tensions between the Kurds and the Arab-led government in Baghdad. There is a fundamental conflict of interest between the central government and the KRG:

Baghdad sees Kurdish autonomy and independence as undermining its power and sovereignty, while the KRG's quest for independence makes any Iraqi involvement in Kurdish affairs unwanted. This irreconcilable difference underscores the contentious political disputes between Erbil and Baghdad and has defined Baghdad-Kurdish relations for a century.

Though Iraq's central government has maintained its opposition to Kurdish independence, how Baghdad would react to the establishment of a sovereign Kurdistan depends largely on the manner in which independence occurs. Baghdad would see a unilateral declaration of Kurdish independence as a purposeful effort to undermine the central government's authority, and react in a hostile manner. Baghdad also would oppose KRG independence gained through the collapse of the Iraqi state, but the central government's levers of power to punish the Kurds would be limited. Kurdish independence resulting from a negotiated separation would be the most beneficial to both Baghdad and Erbil, but the possibility of this hypothetical scenario becoming a reality requires a drastic change in the central government's calculus as to what is in Iraq's national interests.

Erbil must consider several factors when deliberating the costs and benefits of becoming independent in the near future. Establishing a sovereign nation is difficult and would be even more challenging if the Kurds faced opposition from the rest of Iraq. Mitigating the adverse consequences and blowback would be a primary concern. Because of this, the Kurds are most likely to seek a separation from Iraq through a negotiated settlement or by fleeing a collapsing or failed state.

The discussion presented here focused mainly on Baghdad's possible responses to Kurdish independence and the impact this would have on the Kurds; however, other factors, such as Tehran and Ankara's support or opposition to independence, would also influence how Baghdad and the Kurds behave in any scenario. The perception of, and reaction to, the emergence of a sovereign Kurdistan cannot be looked at solely in the context of Iraq. Regional dynamics will inevitably be a factor. While Baghdad has a significant stake in Kurdish independence, the interplay between Baghdad, Ankara, and Tehran's interests complicates how the separation of the KRG from the rest of Iraq could play out.

CHAPTER FOUR

Turkey's Reaction to an Independent Kurdistan

Turkey's approach to the KRG has changed dramatically since the period immediately following the overthrow of Saddam Hussein. On the basis of its adamant opposition to Kurdish independence, after the 2003 invasion Ankara resisted any moves by the KRG to become more politically or economically autonomous from Baghdad. In the past decade, however, Turkey has forged close political and commercial ties with the KRG and dropped its fierce opposition to the Kurds' territorial expansion and growing control over northern Iraq's energy resources. Perhaps related to this change in attitude, Erbil has welcomed investments by Turkish companies in the Kurdistan Region, and Turkish firms were among the first to obtain production-sharing concessions to explore for oil in the KRG following the adoption of the Kurdistan Region's oil law in 2007. Ankara—which over time has become the KRG's closest partner in the Middle East—now appears likely to accept the emergence of a sovereign Kurdish state in what is now northern Iraq, although the means by which such a state comes about could affect the extent of Turkey's initial support.

Turkey's change of heart was driven by a combination of internal politics and regional developments. As the Middle East Institute's Gönül Tol wrote in 2014, "Changing regional and domestic dynamics have pushed Turkey to recalibrate its Iraq policy, making the KRG a strategic ally as an alternative source of energy, a buffer against a hostile

Baghdad and Iran, and a partner in Turkey's quest to resolve its Kurdish problem."[1]

In the political sphere, having decided to grant Turkey's own Kurdish population greater political and cultural representation, the Erdoğan government had little reason to fear that Iraqi Kurdish independence would entice Turkey's own Kurdish population to secede. Indeed, a years-long peace process led the Turkish government to allow Kurds to gain greater local autonomy, create avenues for cultural expression, and organize political parties, such as the People's Democratic Party (Halkların Demokratik Partisi, or HDP), that could represent Kurdish interests in national elections—perhaps the ultimate symbol that Kurds are becoming integrated into Turkish politics and society.

Although the internal peace process collapsed in late 2015 after a Kurdish party's electoral successes led Erdoğan to call new elections and oppose Kurdish political mobilization, the crisis did not increase the regime's fears of Kurdish secession. Moreover, although the regime used emergency decrees to remove two dozen Kurdish mayors and purge thousands of Kurdish schoolteachers in the wake of a July 2016 military coup attempt, these steps were undertaken principally to make the movement of exiled opposition figure Fethullah Gulen—whom Erdoğan blamed for the coup attempt—appear more far-reaching than it is, as well as to consolidate the government's control in Kurdish areas. The electoral crisis, the resulting PKK violence, and the coup attempt all provided Erdoğan with opportunities to consolidate his power domestically; none of the incidents altered Erdoğan's view that an independent KRG with close political and commercial ties to Turkey would be a useful political and economic partner.[2]

---

[1] Tol, 2014b, p. 2.

[2] The government of President Recip Tayyip Erdoğan came to see Kurdish political mobilization as a threat once again after the June 2015 parliamentary elections, in which the HDP gained sufficient seats in parliament to deny Erdoğan's Justice and Development Party (AKP) the majority needed to modify the constitution and strengthen presidential powers. Ironically, however, the threat posed by the HDP was not that its electoral showing increased the likelihood that the state would collapse by elevating secession as a political option, but rather that it diluted the AKP's power by institutionalizing the Kurdish-dominated party in the Turkish polity. As a result, although Erdoğan resumed attacks on the PKK and again

In addition, as Turkey's economy expanded rapidly in the years after the U.S.-led invasion of Iraq,[3] Turkey's energy needs increased, and Ankara sought to diversify its supply of energy[4] so as to reduce its dependence on imports from Russia and Iran. As the KRG worked to build pipeline infrastructure, the energy resources of next-door northern Iraq appeared to Turkey as an increasingly tantalizing solution. An independent Kurdistan in northern Iraq may be even freer to sell its hydrocarbon resources than a KRG still dependent on Baghdad's revenue sharing and undermined by Baghdad's international assertion of legal title over the Kurdistan Region's oil deposits.

The Turkish military's changing role in society and its evolving views of the Kurdish conflict were critical to the Turkish government's change of heart on the Kurdish issue. Between 2003 and 2009, Parliament significantly curtailed the military's political influence.[5] Simultaneously, the Turkish armed forces had come to the realization that, after 25 years of fighting, the Kurdish problem was not solvable through military means alone.[6] Moreover, by partnering with the KRG, Ankara could undermine the ability of the rebel PKK[7] to find safe haven in

---

demonized Kurdish parties, including both the HDP and the PKK, so as to strengthen his hand in new elections, the crisis he created does not indicate a fear of Kurdish secession—just the opposite, in fact. The electoral crisis and the resumption of violence thus do not change Turkey's current view that the KRG is a vital regional partner that may well become more useful after independence. See Paul and Seyrek, 2015.

[3] The Turkish economy nearly quadrupled between 2001 and 2012, from $200 billion to almost $800 billion per year (Colombo, 2014). Between 2003 and 2011, Turkey's economy grew at an annual rate of 8 percent or higher except for a 4 percent decline in 2009 (data from Organisation for Economic Co-operation and Development, undated). GDP growth rate plummeted in 2012, and has remained weak since then, as a result of instability in Syria, weak demand in European countries struggling to recover from the global financial crisis, a drop in government-funded construction, and a decline in credit-fueled domestic consumption (Peker and Candemir, 2015; Colombo, 2014).

[4] Republic of Turkey Ministry of Foreign Affairs, undated-b.

[5] Tol, 2014b, p. 3. Also Larrabee, 2010, pp. 103, 106; Tol, 2010.

[6] Barkey, 2010, p. 3.

[7] In 2003, the PKK renamed itself the Kurdistan People's Congress (Kongra-Gel, or KGK). Because it nevertheless continues to be widely referred to as the PKK (particularly in the United States), the group will be referred to as the PKK throughout this chapter.

northern Iraq, hinder the ability of the PKK's Syrian affiliates to establish an autonomous Kurdish zone along the Turkish-Syrian border, and mitigate the risk that Iraqi Kurds would encourage separatism among Kurds in eastern Turkey.

Turkey and the KRG also share regional interests and concerns that have pushed them closer together, particularly as Iraq and Syria have experienced disruptive violence and instability. Both have populations that are overwhelmingly Sunni and generally secular (despite an increasing emphasis on Islam by Turkey's ruling AKP party), and both are oriented principally toward the United States and Europe rather than toward their neighbors in the Middle East. As a result, both Ankara and Erbil are concerned about Iran's efforts to expand its regional influence, Shi'a dominance (and Iranian influence) over the central government in Baghdad, the security implications of the withdrawal of U.S. forces from Iraq, and opposition to ISIL's destabilizing brutality and territorial expansion.[8]

Finally, as the KRG has become more stable and prosperous, Syria has collapsed into civil war and the Iraqi central government has proven to be unable to maintain security in the central and southern parts of the country. Given the rise in instability throughout the Middle East, from Turkey's perspective, Kurdish secession from Iraq would not represent the breakup of Iraq so much as legitimize the establishment of a stable neighbor along its borders that could keep Iraqi violence at bay while both exacerbating divisions among and mitigating the autonomy of Syrian Kurds.[9] The establishment of an independent Iraqi Kurdistan may thus no longer be a threat to Turkish interests. Indeed, as Soner Çağaptay of the Washington Institute for Near East Policy writes, other threats have come to eclipse the prospects of Kurdish independence so much that "it now seems safe to say that if the Iraqi Kurdish regional government declared independence Ankara would be the first capital to recognize it."[10]

---

[8] Larrabee and Tol, 2011, p. 146.

[9] Tocci, 2013, p. 5.

[10] Çağaptay, 2014.

Turkey's Long Opposition to Kurdish Independence

The situation in northern Iraq in 2015 resembles what the International Crisis Group forecasted in 2005 would be "Turkey's nightmare scenario": a dynamic involving "either Iraq's descent into civil war, creation of a Kurdish state in the north, or a combination whereby the Kurds would escape the dissolving center to secure their own region, bring in Kirkuk for reasons of history and economic viability, and establish an independent Kurdistan in fact if not name."[11] Yet as Iraq has experienced an ineffective central government, sectarian violence, and an vicious onslaught from ISIL, Turkey not only has tacitly accepted the KRG's growing autonomy from Baghdad and *de facto* control over Kirkuk, it has developed a close partnership with Kurdish authorities in Erbil. What changed in ten years that Ankara now embraces as a partner an Iraqi Kurdish entity that it previously shunned?

For decades after the collapse of the Ottoman Empire, Turkish leader Mustafa Kemal Atatürk and his successors used the state apparatus to press Kurds, Armenians, Greeks, and other ethnic groups living in Anatolia to assimilate into a secular Turkish culture through a process of "Turkification." Kurdish revolts in the 1920s and 1930s led the state to suppress expressions of Kurdish cultural or linguistic identity. In 1978, inspired by anti-colonial wars of independence and left-wing revolutionaries in other parts of the world, Abdullah Ocalan and other Turkish Marxists established the PKK to create, through an armed insurgency, an independent Greater Kurdistan that would serve as a homeland for Kurds throughout the Middle East. Concerned at the prospects of an armed secessionist movement, the military government that took power in 1980 cracked down further on Kurdish nationalists and banned use of the Kurdish language—steps that further fueled Kurdish nationalism and opposition to the Turkish state.[12]

For most of the intervening three decades, Turkey has seen the predominantly Kurdish areas of northern Iraq as a potential wellspring of Kurdish nationalism, which the U.S. Iraq Study Group described

---

[11] International Crisis Group, 2005.

[12] Barkey and Fuller, 1998, pp. 9–17; Fevzi and Sarihan, 2013, pp. 64–67.

in its 2006 report as "an existential threat to Turkey's own internal stability."[13] In the mid-1990s, in the wake of the 1991 Gulf War that enabled Iraqi Kurdish parties to run their own affairs more or less free from Baghdad's interference, Turkey launched extended cross-border assaults into northern Iraq to root out safe havens used by PKK fighters. Such operations continued into the late 2000s, even well after the overthrow of Saddam Hussein led to the establishment of an autonomous KRG in the Iraqi provinces of Dohuk, Erbil, and Sulaimaniyah.

Throughout this 30-year period, Turkey saw Iraqi Kurdistan as a haven for PKK fighters, a wellspring of Kurdish nationalism that could fuel Turkey's internal rebellion, and, at worst, an inspiration for Turkish Kurds to secede from Turkey and join an irredentist Kurdish state proclaimed by Iraqi Kurdish leaders. An independent Iraqi Kurdistan made prosperous by its natural resources would, many Turkish officials feared, be an embarrassing contrast to the widespread poverty in Turkey's Kurdish regions and encourage Turkish Kurds to secede.[14] Turkey thus worked aggressively to prevent Iraqi Kurds from taking actions that could be seen as steps toward eventual independence. It expressed vehement opposition, for example, to the movement of Kurdish peshmerga into Kirkuk as Saddam's army retreated during the U.S. invasion in 2003; sought to delay the implementation of a referendum on Kirkuk's status as called for under Article 140 of the Iraqi Constitution until the city's Kurdish, Turkmen, and Arab communities agreed on how to proceed;[15] and even objected strenuously to the use of the term "Kurdistan" to refer to northern Iraq.[16]

Turkey's Change of Heart

In the mid-2000s, Ankara's approach to Kurdish independence changed fairly rapidly. A decade after suggesting that vital Turkish

---

[13] Baker et al., 2006.

[14] International Crisis Group, 2005.

[15] Gözkaman, 2013.

[16] "Brawl Erupts over Word 'Kurdistan' in Turkish Parliament," 2013.

interests would be threatened by Kurdish rule in Kirkuk, senior Turkish officials expressed only tepid affirmations of Iraqi territorial integrity when Kurdish peshmerga actually moved into Kirkuk in June 2014 in the face of a threatened ISIL assault and in the context of the headlong flight of the defending ISF forces.[17] A ruling party spokesperson asserted that Kurdish independence would no longer be a *casus belli*.[18] Turkey is not, however, standing by passively while the KRG strengthens its case for independence; it appears to be actively empowering the KRG to be more politically and economically assertive. Indeed, Nathalie Tocci, of the Istituto Affari Internazionali, argues, "Relations between Turkey and Northern Iraq have evolved at a breathtaking pace, with Turkish policies currently bolstering the KRG's drift towards independence, a prospect considered unthinkable in Ankara only a few years ago."[19] After years of close interactions to advance mutual interests, KRG President Masoud Barzani expressed his belief that although Turkey might not assist the emergence of an independent Kurdistan, neither would Ankara oppose it.[20]

Ankara's change of heart stemmed from changes to both its domestic and foreign policies. Domestically, the government's decision to seek a resolution of the internal conflict with the PKK, along with the PKK's decision to pursue greater political and cultural rights within the Turkish political system, mitigated the threat of irredentist nationalism from northern Iraq. Although the Turkish government brought an end to the peace process and resumed the military conflict with the PKK after the June 2015 elections, this policy change is widely seen as an attempt to bolster the AKP's nationalist credentials, demonstrate that Erdoğan is sufficiently strong to protect Turks from instability and chaos, and undermine (if not eliminate) the HDP's representation in parliament through the calling of new elections[21]—during which the

---

[17] Çağaptay, 2014.

[18] Dombey, 2014.

[19] Tocci, 2013.

[20] Baydar, 2014.

[21] Paul and Seyrek, 2015. See also Tharoor, 2015; Henley, Shaheen, and Letsch, 2015.

party met the 10 percent threshold for parliamentary representation but won 25 percent fewer seats[22]—not as a decision that Kurdish separatism is once again something to fear.

Ankara and Erbil also sought closer relations as a result of a confluence of foreign policy interests, particularly their mutual desire to insulate themselves from the political dysfunction and violence caused by Iraq's increasing sectarianism, contain instability created by the Syrian civil war, exploit the KRG's oil resources, and undermine competing Kurdish groups in both Turkey and Syria. Moreover, Turkish leaders appear to have concluded, according to University of Exeter professor Gareth Stansfield, that being an active partner in the KRG's path to independence will enable Ankara to shape and influence its emerging neighbor in ways that advance Turkey's interests.[23]

Domestic Politics

Throughout the 1980s and 1990s, years of PKK attacks drove the then military-dominated Turkish government to view the Kurdish problem as a security challenge to be managed with military tools. This "heavily securitised policy response . . . hindered successive Turkish governments in their efforts to develop a comprehensive approach to the issue that integrated political, economic, social and psychological factors."[24] Use of the Kurdish language and any form of Kurdish cultural expression were prohibited and severely punished.

By the end of the 1990s, the groundwork had been laid for both the PKK and the Turkish government to pursue nonmilitary solutions. After being arrested in 1999, PKK leader Abdullah Öcalan called from prison for the PKK to seek equality within a democratic but unified Turkey rather than an independent or autonomous Kurdish region[25]— a decision that was welcomed by many war-weary Kurds and Turks

---

[22] Akyol, 2015.

[23] Stansfield, 2014.

[24] Larrabee and Tol, 2011.

[25] Gunter, 2000, pp. 854–856.

alike.[26] In 2003, in part to bolster its prospects for membership in the European Union, Turkey passed laws that permitted greater use of the Kurdish language, which enabled Kurds to express their grievances more widely and fostered interaction among Kurdish political groups.[27]

During the same period, the role of the Turkish military in politics diminished,[28] which reduced the government's tendency to present Kurdish issues solely as security challenges and opened the door to political solutions to the Kurdish conflict.[29] The military had long been a defender of the Kemalist ideology underpinning the modern Turkish state, which promoted a Turkish nationalism in which ethnic minorities, including Kurds, were pressured to assimilate.[30] From the military's point of view, Kurdish nationalism was a threat not only to the country's national identity, but also to its territorial integrity. However, in 2003, Parliament increased civilian control over the military, in part by reducing the authority of the military-dominated National Security Council and by diluting the military's influence over it.[31] The military's influence was further weakened in 2007, when it issued a thinly veiled threat to stage a coup to prevent the AKP from consolidating its power in parliamentary elections. The party won an overwhelming victory— a result that was widely seen as a rebuke to the military—and the military failed to follow through on its threat.[32] In 2009, the AKP reined in the military further by placing it more firmly under the civilian judiciary; Parliament abolished military courts' jurisdiction over civilians and placed military officers under the jurisdiction of civilian courts.[33] In 2010, then–Prime Minister Erdoğan asserted the civilian government's authority to appoint officers to senior-level military positions, a

---

[26] Kinzer, 1999.

[27] Werz and Hoffman, 2014, p. 13.

[28] Tol, 2014b, p. 2.

[29] Tol, 2014b, p. 12. Also Larrabee and Tol, 2011, p. 145.

[30] Larrabee, 2010, pp. 91–92.

[31] Larrabee, 2010, p. 103.

[32] Tol, 2010.

[33] Larrabee, 2010, p. 106.

privilege long claimed by the military leadership.[34] The diminished role of the military in Turkish politics created political space for Turks to address the status of Kurds at the ballot box and to treat it as a political question rather than as a security threat.

In mid-2009, the pro-Kurdish Democratic Society Party (Demokratik Toplum Partisi, or DTP) defeated the ruling AKP party in local elections in southeastern Turkey,[35] with Kurdish voters making clear that cultural and linguistic issues were their primary interest. The AKP responded with concessions in what was known as the "Kurdish opening."[36] In 2012, Öcalan called from prison for the PKK to end its armed struggle. In March 2013, Turkey and the PKK agreed on a ceasefire and engaged in peace talks. Although the peace process collapsed in the wake of the June 2015 elections, in which the AKP lost its legislative majority and the Kurdish-dominated HDP secured representation in parliament—a development described below—the resumption of the conflict appeared to be a short-term security crisis engineered by the AKP to help it regain its majority in a subsequent election scheduled for five months later.

As Kurdish political demands became more moderate, and as the increasingly civilian-dominated Turkish government[37] came to see the country's Kurds as a political constituency rather than an internal security threat, Ankara began to have less to fear from any irredentist nationalism originating from Iraqi Kurdistan, which enabled it to view the KRG as a potential partner rather than as a destabilizing influence.

Turkey's Energy Needs

Turkey's economy has grown at a rapid pace, expanding an average of 5.5 percent annually from 2004 to 2014.[38] As a result, its energy

---

[34] Tol, 2010.

[35] Jenkins, 2009.

[36] Larrabee and Tol, 2011, p. 147.

[37] Turkey's military dominated the nation's politics from the time it launched a coup in 1980 until the early 2000s, when the AKP began a process of civilianization designed to improve the country's bid for European Union membership. See Satana, 2014; Aslan, 2011.

[38] Kottasova, 2014.

demand has grown faster than any country in the world except China,[39] expanding at 6 to 8 percent per year.[40] Turkey's natural gas consumption tripled from 15 billion cubic meters (bcm) in 2000 to 46 bcm a decade later.[41] "In order to sustain its economic growth" and satisfy its energy requirements, writes Tol, "Ankara wants to strengthen its energy security, ensure diversification of suppliers, and establish itself as an energy hub between the energy-producing countries to its east and the energy-consuming countries to its west."[42]

Turkey is heavily dependent on oil and gas imports from Russia and Iran, both of which provide extensive support to the Assad regime in Damascus. As a result, Ankara may feel pressure to withhold support from anti-Assad fighters so as to avoid antagonizing its energy suppliers. Diversifying its sources of energy resources could provide greater energy security, reduce energy costs, and, by reducing Turkey's reliance on Russia and Iran, enable Turkey to be more aggressive in Syria.[43] Neighboring Iraqi Kurdistan—rich in oil and gas and dependent on land routes across Turkey for exports—is an appealing energy partner. In 2013, Turkey and the KRG agreed to construct new pipelines with the capacity to export 2 million barrels of oil per day and 10 bcm of natural gas per day from the Kurdistan Region to Turkey.[44] The KRG Ministry of Natural Resources announced in January 2016 that it would begin exporting natural gas to Turkey in 2019 or 2020.[45]

Regional Security Concerns

Ankara, like Erbil, has felt threatened by the sectarian violence and political divisions fostered by former Iraqi Prime Minister Nouri Maliki. In 2014, a spokesperson for the AKP equated the chaos in Iraq

---

[39] Arango and Krauss, 2013.

[40] Tol, 2013.

[41] Tanchum, 2015a.

[42] Tol, 2013.

[43] Tol, 2013.

[44] See Pamuk and Coskun, 2013.

[45] Razzouk, 2016.

with Shi'a dominance in Baghdad, stating that the United States "didn't bring peace, stability, unity, they just left chaos, widows, orphans. They created a Shia bloc to the south of our country."[46] Turkey has worked diligently to counter Shi'a control. It has supported Sunni political parties;[47] given safe haven to Iraq's Sunni vice president, Tareq Hashemi, after Prime Minister Maliki sought his arrest;[48] and provided military support to anti-ISIL Sunni militias as a way of balancing the growth of Shi'a militias, most of whom receive support from Tehran.[49]

In addition to opposing the emergence of a strong Shi'a-dominated government in Baghdad, Turkey has also had concerns about Iran's growing sway on the Maliki government and in Iraq as a whole. Broadly speaking, Ankara and Tehran see each other as rivals for regional dominance, which they seek to promote through Sunni and Shi'a partners, respectively.[50] Indeed, the Turkish government is suspicious of Iranian influence along and even inside its borders, given Tehran's support for the Shi'a in Iraq, the Assad regime in Syria, and PKK rebels fighting in Turkey.[51] Through close relations with the KRG that involved political, economic, and security cooperation, Turkey could help inoculate neighboring Iraqi Kurdistan from both instability and creeping Iranian influence.[52]

Syria

Turkey has also seen the KRG as a potential partner in an effort to prevent the PKK's Syrian affiliate from establishing an autonomous zone on the Turkish border. The Assad regime effectively ceded control over the predominantly Kurdish regions in the north to the Democratic Union Party (PYD), the PKK's Syrian affiliate, so it could con-

---

[46] Dombey, 2014

[47] Taştekin, 2013.

[48] "Iraq's Fugitive VP Not to Return to Iraq: Turkey," 2012.

[49] Zeidan, 2015.

[50] Kane, 2011.

[51] Kuru, 2012. Also Gafarli, 2015; Qurbani, 2015.

[52] Stansfield, 2014, p. 8.

centrate its efforts elsewhere. Even while professing a desire to preserve Syrian unity (perhaps in part to avoid antagonizing Ankara), the PYD has sought to administer Kurdish areas as a semi-autonomous enclave; it established parallel ministries and legislative institutions, provided utility services independently, and even switched signs and school textbooks to Latin (rather than Arabic) letters.[53] These steps to promote administrative and cultural autonomy in Syrian Kurdish areas resemble the ways in which the KRG gradually established a bureaucracy and a Kurdish political/cultural identity that was distinct from that of the rest of Iraq.

Turkey has come to fear the PYD's administration of these Kurdish-led areas,[54] which could serve as a safe haven from which PKK forces could attack Turkey and resume the Kurdish insurgency.[55] Indeed, when Assad's forces withdrew from northeastern Syria in July 2012, "Ankara feared that it was witnessing the birth of a PKK-led state on its doorstep," according to Soner Çağaptay.[56] As the conflict in northern Syria heated up in 2015 and 2016, Turkey has attacked PYD positions in Syria[57] and is believed to have provided support to ISIS fighters combating the group. As Amberin Zaman writes, "Fears of a PKK-led Kurdish entity [in Syria] are so deeply engrained that the AKP may feel more comfortable co-habiting with ISIS than with the people best equipped to beat them."[58]

Although Turkey has actively fought the PYD's ability to establish an autonomous Kurdish zone along the Syrian-Turkish border, it has taken steps to demonstrate that its anti-PYD actions should not be interpreted as anti-Kurdish hostility. Amberin Zaman notes that "on August 23, a day before Turkish troops entered Syria for the first time to fight ISIS—and the YPG—Barzani traveled to Ankara to meet with

---

[53] Hoppe et al., 2014.

[54] Hoppe et al., 2014; Jenkins, 2014.

[55] Werz and Hoffman, 2014. Also Tocci, 2013, p. 71.

[56] Çağaptay, 2014.

[57] Barkey, 2016.

[58] Zaman, 2016a.

Erdoğan and other Turkish leaders, thus allowing Turkey to show that its actions against the YPG did not target all Kurds."[59] A week later, Erdoğan foreign policy advisor İbrahim Kalın went to great pains to emphasize that Turkey's military intervention was not aimed at Kurds:

> The Euphrates Shield Operation is against the presence of the DAESH and other terror organizations [such as the PYD]. We strongly condemn efforts to present this operation as being against Syrian Kurds and their achievements. Turkey has no problem with the Syrian Kurds. Turkey has no problems with Kurds in Turkey, Kurds in Iraq, Kurds in Iran, and Kurds in the region or in any part of the world.[60]

The Erdoğan-Barzani meeting and related statements appear intended to reassure the KRG that Turkey's intervention to prevent the establishment of a Kurdish enclave in Syria does not reflect a change of heart regarding the status of the Kurdish enclave in Iraq.

Indeed, Iraqi Kurds remain a crucial partner for Turkey as it attempts to undermine the PYD and its PKK allies. Even before Turkey took military action in Syria, it sought to pull northern Syria into Ankara's political and economic orbit, as it did over time with Iraqi Kurds, to minimize the ability of the PKK to maintain a potential base of operations in a PYD-dominated zone along the Turkish frontier.[61] To assist with these efforts, Ankara has looked to Erbil, which similarly views the PYD—a Kurdish group with an independent political base and an armed militia—as a potential rival.[62] Stephen Larrabee notes that KRG President Barzani is working to bolster alternatives to the PYD in Syria, who would then become dependent on Erbil and thereby subject to Turkey's influence:

---

[59] Zaman, 2016b, p. 19.

[60] "Turkey 'Targets PYD, Not Kurds' in Syria," 2016.

[61] Larrabee, 2013, pp. 133–146

[62] Pollack, 2014. Also Park, 2014.

In northern Iraq, Barzani is training Kurdish fighters from Syria who he hopes will return home and form the nucleus of a force that will rival the PYD's popular protection units. The force is intended to help secure the autonomy of the Kurdish areas of Syria, much as the peshmerga have done in northern Iraq. Barzani's efforts represent a more moderate solution to the Kurdish problem. They seek to establish an autonomous Kurdish entity similar to KRG-controlled Iraq by fostering economic interdependence, developing cross-border trade and investment, and building energy links with Turkey. They are viewed positively by Ankara because they do not support an assertive, destabilizing Kurdish entity seeking full independence. The PKK, by contrast, views Barzani's increasing influence among the Kurds with concern.[63]

Although Turkey has opposed any form of pan-Kurdish irredentism,[64] it appears to be encouraging (or at least tolerating) a form of Kurdish nationalism in which the KRG is able to offer protection and support to its Syrian brethren. Rather than promote Kurdish identity, of course, Turkey is interested principally in ensuring that if northern Syria is, in fact, to be a semi-autonomous Kurdish zone, its leaders should have close ties to Ankara's allies in Erbil and include as few PKK-aligned figures as possible. "With Syria ablaze," writes Tocci, "the KRG is the most critical partner to ensure that Syria's centrifugal forces are brought into Turkey's orbit, that the PKK ceasefire holds and that Kurdish secessionism in Turkey's southeast is kept at bay."[65] Ankara would not tolerate an internationally recognized Kurdish region in Syria, but it is apparently willing to accept a *de facto* Syrian Kurdish self-governing area that is calm but not dominated by any particular faction—least of all the PYD. Currently, the PYD-dominated areas along the Turkish border are fragmented (see Figure 4.1), which limits the ability of Syrian Kurds to consolidate their control and forces them to expend resources on supplying and supporting noncontiguous

---

[63] Larrabee, 2013, p. 141.

[64] Tocci, 2013, p. 71.

[65] Tocci, 2013, pp. 74–75.

Figure 4.1
Areas Controlled by Syrian Kurds and Other Factions
(as of August 2015)

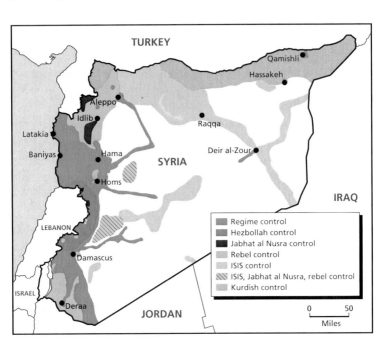

SOURCE: Institute for the Study of War. Used with permission.
RAND *RR1452-4.1*

territories. Turkey is unlikely to accept a consolidated YPG-dominated area along the length of its border. Thus, as long as Syrian Kurds are able to administer a semi-autonomous territory along Turkey's borders, Ankara will remain reliant on Erbil to advance its interests there by supporting groups outside the PYD umbrella. If Erbil decides to pursue independence, it will likely use its influence in Syria as a point of leverage to secure Turkish recognition of its sovereignty.

Resumed Fighting After the June 2015 Election Did Not Change AKP's Calculus on Iraqi Kurdish Independence

One month after the June 2015 elections, in response to an attack on a Turkish police station, the Turkish government declared an end to the Kurdish peace process and resumed military strikes on the PKK.

Although President Erdoğan and other Turkish officials blamed the resumption of the conflict on the PKK, many observers suggest that the crisis was manufactured by the Erdoğan regime to reverse its electoral loss, which would suggest that the government's views on Iraqi Kurdish independence had not changed.[66]

Campaigning for the June 2015 parliamentary election, President Erdoğan called on Turks to give the AKP a parliamentary supermajority of 400 seats so that the party could write a new constitution that would strengthen presidential power.[67] The HDP, a Kurdish-dominated coalition of leftist political parties that offered a progressive alternative to the increasingly authoritarian AKP,[68] foiled his plans. The AKP suffered its worst electoral defeat since it took power in 2002, failing to secure a majority and losing 69 parliamentary seats.[69] The HDP won 80 out of 550 parliamentary seats,[70] representing the first time a Kurdish party crossed the 10 percent threshold needed to secure representation in parliament.[71] The electoral success of the HDP prevented the AKP from securing the two-thirds majority needed for President Erdoğan to unilaterally modify the constitution and strengthen presidential powers. As Council on Foreign Relations Senior Fellow Steven Cook writes, "AKP's loss of seats is a rejection of Erdoğan's moves to centralize power and hollow out Turkey's political institutions."[72] Turkish journalist-author Cengiz Çandar makes clear that Erdoğan's plans were foiled specifically by the HDP's success, noting that "the parliamentary arithmetic the HDP has created deprives [Erdoğan] of all [his] calculations."[73]

---

[66] Paul and Seyrek, 2015.

[67] Idiz, 2015b.

[68] Malik, 2015. See also Patrick Reilly, 2015; Tanchum, 2015b.

[69] Çağaptay, Stull, and Bhaskar, 2015, p. 1.

[70] Letsch and Traynor, 2015.

[71] Çağaptay, Stull, and Bhaskar, 2015, p. 14.

[72] Ricotta, 2015.

[73] Çamlıbel, 2015.

The HDP's success raised the possibility that the ruling party might need to partner with a Kurdish-led bloc to form a government or pass key legislation.[74] The Kurdish party's surprising degree of popularity symbolized the dramatic change in political status for Turkey's Kurds—from outlaw to potential kingmaker in 15 years. Instead, AKP leaders failed—some would say refused—to reach an agreement to form a coalition government, which thus required new elections.[75] President Erdoğan, Prime Minister Davutoğlu, and other AKP officials took a range of steps designed to cause support for the HDP to fall below the 10 percent threshold—steps that would not have been necessary, President Erdoğan told Turkish media, "if a party had managed to secure 400 deputies or a number that could change the constitution."[76] In addition to resuming bombings of PKK bases in northern Iraq, Deputy Prime Minister Yalçın Akdoğan disparaged the HDP as "an open supporter, extension and political branch" of the PKK;[77] prosecutors attempted to lift the parliamentary immunity of HDP chair Selahattin Demirtaş, accusing him of support for a terrorist group;[78] and mobs burned down HDP offices in 56 provinces and districts throughout the country.[79] It is clear, according to Tol, that "Erdoğan is hoping to recapture the nationalist votes that the AKP lost in June by cracking down on the PKK."[80]

This strategy worked to a large degree. The resumption of violence between the government and the PKK enabled AKP to draw votes from Turkish nationalist parties and from liberal HDP supporters with concerns about its ties to the PKK. As a result, although the HDP still

---

[74] Zaman, 2015a. See also Idiz, 2015a.

[75] Fifty-seven percent of Turks believed that Erdoğan was responsible for the failure to reach agreement on a coalition government, essentially concluding that the president was seeking a "do-over" election. See "Most Turks See Erdoğan as Culprit in Failure of Coalition Talks," 2015.

[76] Idiz, 2015b.

[77] "Deputy PM Akdoğan Strikes Back at HDP, Calls It 'Extension' of PKK," 2015.

[78] O'Byrne, 2015.

[79] Tol, 2015.

[80] Tol, 2015a.

managed to cross the 10 percent threshold necessary for parliamentary representation, it secured only 61 seats as opposed to the 80 seats it had won in June. The AKP increased its share of the vote by 8.5 percent, which enabled it to form a government without having to enter into a coalition.[81]

Although PKK anti-government violence has continued long after the November 2015 election, the AKP-led government does not appear to want to resume a long-running war with the PKK. Indeed, according to Soner Çağaptay of the Washington Institute for Near East Studies, "the country appears to be experiencing a period of controlled conflict, with neither the PKK nor the government aiming for full-scale war."[82] It therefore seems unlikely that the AKP has re-adopted the view that Kurdish nationalism poses an existential threat to the country, which would suggest that it continues to see little irredentist threat from a thriving independent Kurdistan in northern Iraq.

Erdoğan has, however, taken opportunities to concentrate his power at the Kurds' expense. After a small group of military officers attempted to overthrow the government in July 2016, Erdoğan purged and jailed government officials, military officers, and even teachers linked to the exiled opposition figure Fethullah Gulen, a longtime political rival whom Erdoğan blamed for the coup attempt.[83] Alleging ties between the PKK and the Gulen movement,[84] in September 2016 the government purged 11,000 teachers[85] and issued an emergency decree to replace two dozen elected mayors and members of parliament in Kurdish areas[86] whom Interior Minister Suleyman Soylu inferred were taking their instructions from the PKK.[87]

---

[81] Akyol, 2015.

[82] For its part, Çağaptay writes, the PKK seems interested in strengthening its own position vis-à-vis the HDP. See Çağaptay, 2015.

[83] "Purges Since Coup Attempt in Turkey Shake Higher Education," 2016.

[84] Aktan, 2016.

[85] Gursel, 2016. See also Kucuksahin, 2016.

[86] Gurcan, 2016. Also Kucuksahin, 2016.

[87] Gursel, 2016.

Should the controlled conflict lead to lasting violence, however, both domestic reconciliation with Turkish Kurds and the détente between Turkey and the KRG may be undermined. Although Erbil does not approve of Turkey's unilateral air strikes on PKK camps in its territory, it does little to object. However, an extended period of Turkish bombardment could generate greater sympathy for the PKK fighters among the KRG's population and drive the KRG to reduce its own efforts to rein in PKK activities. Similarly, an extended military campaign could cause Turkish Kurds to reevaluate their willingness to participate in the Turkish polity rather than separate from it. In such a case, Turkish Kurds may once again look to PKK guerrillas, rather than to HDP politicians, to advance their interests, which could give rise to a renewed full-scale Kurdish insurgency.[88]

As a result, although the AKP leadership appears to intend the counterinsurgency campaign to be short-lived, the resumption of a long-term internal conflict could alienate Turkey's Kurdish population and drive a wedge between Ankara and its allies in Erbil. Such developments could drive Turkish leaders to once again fear the power of irredentist Kurdish nationalism, which could create misgivings regarding Iraqi Kurdish independence.

Turkish Policies Promote KRG Autonomy and Eventual Independence

As Turkey's internal political and economic environment changed, it became clear that a stable, prosperous Iraqi Kurdistan could be an asset to Ankara's domestic policies and regional interests. In pursuit of its own strategic interests, Turkey has engaged the Iraqi Kurds in a range of ways that have bolstered the KRG's autonomy within the Iraqi polity, its economic strength, and its military capabilities—all of which have made the KRG better positioned to pursue independence. As Gareth Stansfield suggested in July 2014, then–Prime Minister Erdoğan saw

---

[88] Çamlıbel, 2015. See also Odendahl, 2015; Tol, 2015.

a strong security rationale in being in close cooperation with the Kurds of Iraq. Being the Iraqi Kurds' "big brother" at a time when they would be making the sensitive transition from federal region of Iraq to either a state of an unstable confederacy or to being an independent Republic would give Ankara the opportunity to ensure that whatever did emerge on Turkey's south-east border would be something, ultimately, that Turkey could not only live with, but control economically and influence politically.[89]

Political Initiatives
Cooperation to Rein in the PKK
Turkey had long demanded that Iraq (including the KRG) take action against PKK havens in northern Iraq, but it was not until the late 2000s that the KRG began to do so in earnest, in large part to make itself a more valuable partner to Turkey.

In October 2008, as Turkey was bombing PKK locations in northern Iraq, Turkish officials demanded that the KRG take action against PKK camps and dismantle the group's communications lines.[90] Kurdish officials indicated that their assistance would be predicated on closer political engagement with Ankara. Iraqi Army chief of staff Lt. Gen. Babakir Zebari, a Kurd and a member of Barzani's KDP,[91] stated that the issue of "PKK bases in northern Iraq can only be solved if Turkey establishes ties with the regional administration. Barzani would respond positively to every measure taken against the PKK if the Turkish government established a dialogue with him."[92]

In late March 2009, Turkish President Abdullah Gul visited Baghdad—the first visit by a Turkish head of state to Iraq in 30 years. During his trip, Turkey, Baghdad, and Erbil agreed to cooperate tri-laterally against the PKK. Iraqi President Jalal Talabani called on the

---

[89] Stansfield, 2014, p. 7.

[90] Ahmed, 2012, pp. 163–164.

[91] Cole, 2010.

[92] Quoted in Ahmed, 2012, pp. 163–164.

PKK to "lay down its arms or leave our territory"[93]—a groundbreaking statement that, Stephen Larrabee and Gönül Tol assert, "was an indication that KRG officials were ready to take stronger action against the PKK, a long-standing Turkish demand and precondition for improved relations."[94] Indeed, Gul commented during his trip that the Kurdish commitment was a sea change in Kurdish policy, demonstrating a view "that winning over Turkey is an advantage. . . . [I]t is the first time I see them doing something [against the PKK]. . . . We are in a new era now."[95] The day after agreeing to collaborate against the PKK, Gul met with KRG Prime Minister Nechirvan Barzani in a first-ever meeting between a Turkish president and an official of the KRG—a significant symbolic recognition of Kurdish sovereignty.[96]

Since Gul's 2009 visit, the KRG has taken a range of steps to weaken the PKK; it has, Tol writes, "banned pro-PKK political parties, arrested PKK politicians, closed down PKK offices, and closely monitors pro-PKK activities"[97]—steps that have significantly endeared Erbil to the Turkish government and demonstrated to Ankara the value of continued close cooperation with the KRG. Erbil's willingness to crack down on the PKK was a critical precondition for Ankara's subsequent political and economic engagement.

Diplomatic Engagement

In October 2009—six months after Gul's visit to Baghdad and five months after Ankara announced that its foreign policy would be based on a strategy of having "zero problems with neighbors"[98]—Turkish Foreign Minister Ahmet Davutoğlu visited Erbil, a step that opened the door to a series of additional high-level contacts and engagement

---

[93] Quoted in "'Disarm or Leave Iraq' Says Iraq's Talabani to PKK," 2009.

[94] Larrabee and Tol, 2011, p. 145.

[95] Quoted in "'Disarm or Leave Iraq' Says Iraq's Talabani to PKK," 2009.

[96] Ahmed, 2012, p. 176.

[97] Tol, 2013.

[98] Republic of Turkey, Ministry of Foreign Affairs, undated-a.

between Turkey and the KRG.[99] In April 2010, KRG President Masoud Barzani traveled to Ankara for meetings with the Turkish president, prime minister, and foreign minister.[100] In March 2010, Turkey opened a consulate in Erbil,[101] enabling routine, ongoing diplomatic engagement between Turkey and the KRG; Prime Minister Erdoğan himself cut the ribbon at the consulate's official opening during an official visit to Erbil a year later in March 2011.[102] By late 2014, Turkey had posted 150 diplomats to Erbil—more than it had stationed in Baghdad—and had opened a consulate in Mosul and a diplomatic "office" in Kirkuk.[103]

Undermining Baghdad's Influence

Since the establishment of Iraq's first post-Saddam government, the KRG has been highly dependent on payments from Baghdad for its operations. As noted earlier, Baghdad and Erbil had agreed in 2004 that the KRG would be entitled to 17 percent of Iraq's oil revenues after deduction of sovereign expenses, though Baghdad frequently withheld these payments or provided less than Erbil calculated it was owed. Although the KRG has been eager to sell its oil resources so as to earn additional revenue, disputes with Baghdad over ownership of the oil have hampered its ability to do so. As Baghdad became a less reliable political and economic partner, Erbil looked increasingly to Turkey, which was happy to supplant Baghdad as the leading external actor in the Kurdistan Region.

In its quest for additional influence over Erbil after 2008, the Turkish government from time to time helped pay KRG government salaries, loaned it funds, purchased Kurdish oil for domestic consumption, and stored additional Kurdish oil until international buyers could

---

[99] Park, 2014.

[100] Park, 2014.

[101] Turkish Consulate General in Erbil, undated-a. See also Turkish Consulate General in Erbil, undated-b; Fielding-Smith, 2010.

[102] "Barzani and Erdoğan Open Erbil Int'l Airport and Turkish Consulate," 2011.

[103] Comments by KRG official, Washington, D.C., November 14, 2014.

be found. As the National Defense University's Denise Natali writes, "Turkey has become the KRG's new financial patron."[104]

Turkey's decision to support the KRG (particularly with oil purchases) risks undermining Ankara's political and economic relations with Baghdad. Indeed, in response to Ankara's decision to purchase Kurdish oil, Iraqi Prime Minister Maliki banned the Turkish state oil company from bidding on exploration deals in southern Iraq.[105] Nevertheless, even if faced with a choice between Iraq or an independent Kurdistan, Ankara would likely choose to sacrifice its ties to Baghdad in order to continue developing relations with Erbil. While Turkey is not eager to alienate Baghdad, it appears to see sufficient economic potential in the KRG to compensate for lost trade with central and southern Iraq. Perhaps more crucially, at a time when Ankara sees the central government in Baghdad as an increasingly less reliable partner, Turkish assistance to the KRG allows it to shape the priorities of the Kurdistan Region on its border and, through it, the viability of Kurdish groups in eastern Turkey and Syria. Making the KRG economically dependent on Ankara is likely to generate political payoffs as well as economic ones for Turkey.

Acquiescence to KRG Territorial Expansion

For years, Turkey made clear that the Kurds should not attempt to expand their territorial holdings, particularly to the city of Kirkuk—formally outside of the KRG's jurisdiction but long prized by Kurds—whose oil resources would greatly facilitate the emergence of an economically viable independent Kurdish state.[106] When Kurdish peshmerga moved into Kirkuk and other disputed areas in 2003 as the Iraqi Army retreated in the face of the U.S. invasion, Turkey secured a commitment from the United States that the Kurds would not hold the captured territory.[107] In February 2005, Turkish General Staff Deputy Chief General İlker Başbuğ implicitly threatened military action

---

[104] Natali, 2014.

[105] Tocci, 2013, p. 70.

[106] Park, 2014, p. 8.

[107] "Kurds to Be Removed from Kirkuk over Turkey Anger," 2003.

if the Kurds took the city, stating, "The Kurdish administration of Kirkuk would be the first step towards the establishment of a Kurdish state. . . . In such a situation, Kirkuk would become a security problem for Turkey. Kirkuk's status is of vital importance for Turkey."[108]

As Turkish relations with the KRG improved and as dialogue with Turkish Kurds made the prospect of Iraqi Kurdish independence less threatening, Ankara has had less to fear from Kurdish territorial expansion. By June 2014, when Iraqi Army forces disintegrated in the force of ISIL's onslaught, Turkey saw little reason to object when Kurdish forces filled the void and stopped ISIL's advance. Roughly 30,000 Kurdish fighters moved into Kirkuk and other areas populated mostly by Kurds, securing large amounts of territory claimed by both Erbil and Baghdad.[109] A Turkish Foreign Ministry official voiced an objection to the KRG's occupation of Kirkuk, asserting, "Turkey's policy with regard to Kirkuk is clear. The city should be governed with a formula agreed upon by all the ethnic groups of Kirkuk. We are against one group of people of Kirkuk dominating others and unilaterally enforcing its solution by military power."[110]

Despite this sentiment, however, Turkey took no actions to reverse the Kurds' territorial expansion. In fact, Soner Çağaptay stated in an interview with National Public Radio,

> Seeing that ISIL could sweep into Kirkuk and take it over, Turkey was now not only comfortable—I'm told behind the scenes that it was actually supportive of the Kurds annexation of Kirkuk. And that suggests that Turkey sees that this is the path to gradual Kurdish secession and is not uncomfortable with those steps.[111]

Indeed, in May 2015—almost a year after the KRG took effective control of Kirkuk and other disputed territories—the Turkish govern-

---

[108] Quoted in Jenkins, 2005.

[109] Filkins, 2014.

[110] Quoted in Arslan, 2014.

[111] "Crowded by Two Shaky States, Turkey Shifts Its Weight in Policy," 2014.

ment sought to open a Turkish consulate in Kirkuk—not something it would do if it objected to Kurdish governance of the city.[112]

Abandoning Iraqi Turkmen

Turkey long has advocated for the rights of Iraqi Turkmen, an ethnic Turkic people living in Kurdish areas. Ankara has provided extensive support to Iraqi Turkmen political parties[113] and to Turkmen militia groups, who have in turn provided access and information regarding the Kurdistan Region to Turkey.[114] Turkey's state interest in the Turkmen community's well-being is considered by some to have been manufactured[115] so as to give Ankara a platform to oppose any effort by Kurds to extend their rule over the oil-rich city of Kirkuk, whose population is roughly half Turkmen.[116] (Indeed, the Iraqi Turkmen Front, a coalition of six political parties, is believed to have been created by Turkey in the mid-1990s to undermine Kurdish claims for an independent state in northern Iraq and, after Saddam's overthrow, to argue against the establishment of a Kurdish region.[117]) When a Turkish official threatened to respond to a Kurdish takeover of Kirkuk with force in 2005, he cited Ankara's interest in protecting the city's large Turkmen population—not the fact that the city's oil resources could make an independent Kurdistan economically viable.[118]

Since strengthening its relations with the KRG, however, Ankara has significantly reduced its advocacy for Turkmen interests.[119] When Kurdish peshmerga moved into Kirkuk in June 2014 during the conflict with ISIL, Turkish officials failed to protest. When Turkey provided the KRG with military assistance to fight ISIL, Turkmen leaders

---

[112] "Turkey Wants to Open Consulate Offices in Kirkuk and Basra," 2015.

[113] Dagher, 2008.

[114] Stratfor Global Intelligence, 2008.

[115] Beehner, 2007. Also International Crisis Group, 2005, pp. 9–11.

[116] International Crisis Group, 2005, pp. 9–11.

[117] Strakes, 2009, p. 377.

[118] Jenkins, 2013.

[119] Taştekin, 2014.

expressed concern that their own militias would be increasingly unable to protect the community from either ISIL or Kurdish aggression and requested that they, too, receive assistance from Turkey—a request that Turkey ignored.[120] When Turkmen fled ISIL's advance, Turkey built refugee camps inside Iraq (in Dohuk and Sinjar[121]) and provided humanitarian aid.[122] However, despite having threatened to invade Iraq to protect Turkmen years earlier, Ankara would not let the Turkmen seek refuge in Turkish territory.[123] Instead, Turkmen displaced by ISIL were protected by a KRG whose dominance they had long disparaged.

Having gained influence in Iraqi Kurdistan by partnering with the KRG, Turkey no longer needed to use its asserted concern for the Turkmen community to protect its interests. In fact, by acquiescing to the KRG's occupation of Kirkuk and by helping Kurdish peshmerga protect Turkmen refugees, Turkey bolstered the KRG's claims to sovereignty over both the disputed city and the Kurdistan Region's Turkmen population.

Economic Initiatives

By encouraging trade and investment with the KRG—and particularly by enabling the export of Kurdish oil and gas—Turkish-facilitated economic growth has enhanced the prospects for an economically viable independent Kurdistan. The potential risks to Turkey of such an outcome have clearly been mitigated, however, by several dynamics. First, Turkey stood to reap significant economic benefits from fostering bilateral trade and investment, including the potential for economic growth in the southeastern part of Turkey that could mitigate the PKK's appeal to disaffected Turkish Kurds living in poverty in the area.[124] Second,

---

[120] "Tuz Khurmatu Turkmen Take Up Arms in Fight Against ISIL," 2014.

[121] Erkuş, 2014a.

[122] Yezdani, 2014.

[123] Erkuş, 2014a.

[124] Jenkins, 2013.

the potential for economic growth in the KRG could help promote security and stability on Turkey's border.[125]

Third, and perhaps most importantly, the lopsided nature of the economic relationship has given Ankara extraordinary political influence over Erbil. Turkey's international trade is highly diversified, whereas the KRG relies on Turkey for the vast majority of its imports and the export of its principal revenue generator, its oil. Instead of fostering economic self-sufficiency, then, Turkey's dominance of the Iraqi Kurdish economy has rendered Erbil heavily dependent on Ankara. Natali argues that Turkey will use this leverage to require the KRG to help it on a range of strategic issues—such as reining in the PKK and the Syrian Kurdish group PYD—as a quid pro quo.[126]

Trade and Investment

As Kurdish per capita GDP rose dramatically—a tenfold (1,000 percent) increase from 2004 to 2011[127]—Turkish companies followed the growing opportunities in Iraqi Kurdistan. The KRG's 2006 investment law encouraged foreign investment and helped promote rapid economic growth in the Kurdistan Region. In the subsequent four years, foreign companies—many of them Turkish—have invested more than $14 billion in the Kurdistan Region.[128] Between 2009 and 2013, the number of Turkish companies registered by the KRG tripled from 485 to almost 1,500—a figure representing roughly three-fifths of all foreign companies in the Kurdistan Region.[129] Turkish companies are involved in most significant sectors of the Kurdish economy, including oil and gas, construction, and banking.[130]

Trade between Turkey and the KRG also skyrocketed. In November 2014, Turkish Foreign Minister Davutoğlu asserted that

---

[125] International Crisis Group, 2005.

[126] Natali, 2014.

[127] World Bank, 2015, p. 19.

[128] Aqrawi, 2010.

[129] Invest in Group, 2013.

[130] Park, 2014, p. 13.

two-thirds of Turkey's total trade with Iraq—$8 billion out of $12 billion—involves the KRG.[131] In 2012, Turkey's exports to the KRG represented 7 percent of Turkey's total exports, making the KRG one of the country's leading markets.[132] In March 2014, Ankara and Erbil announced that five new border crossings would be opened so as to eliminate bottlenecks of goods at the sole official crossing, located in Zakho.[133] Bilateral trade is expected to continue growing, with $20 billion worth of goods flowing between Turkey and the KRG by 2023.[134]

Closer economic and commercial ties are fostering greater interaction among Turkish citizens and KRG residents. In 2012, 25 percent of Erbil International Airport's passengers flew to or from Istanbul (though many of those without question continued onward to other destinations outside Turkey or came to Erbil from other locations). In contrast, however, only 4 percent traveled to/from Baghdad.[135] Between 2006 and 2010, the number of Turkish citizens entering the KRG (mostly for business) almost tripled, from 481,000 to 1.3 million.[136] In highlighting the role that economic cooperation plays in "the strength of our relations," Foreign Minister Davutoğlu stated that more than 100,000 Turkish citizens live and work in the KRG[137]—a figure that would represent roughly 2 percent of the Kurdistan Region's estimated population of 5.1 million.

Oil
Turkey has a strategic interest in developing a reliable supply of oil and gas from northern Iraq, both to ensure adequate energy supplies for its rapidly growing economy and to reduce its dependence on its current

---

[131] "Press Conference by Turkish Prime Minister Ahmet Davutoğlu and KRG President Masoud Barzani," 2014.

[132] Caglayan, 2013.

[133] Dosky, 2014.

[134] Caglayan, 2013.

[135] "Record Growth at Erbil International Airport," 2013.

[136] Çağaptay, Fidan, and Sacikara, 2015.

[137] "Press Conference by Turkish Prime Minister Ahmet Davutoğlu and KRG President Masoud Barzani," 2014.

principal importers, Russia and Iran. The KRG's ability to produce and export its hydrocarbon resources, however, has been undermined by long-standing disputes with Baghdad regarding ownership of the resources—which encompasses the right to sign exploration deals and export contracts—as well as the authority to construct export pipelines and the apportionment of revenues from the sale of the Kurdistan Region's oil and gas. Baghdad has long insisted that all hydrocarbons belong to the federal government, meaning purchasers would pay Baghdad through SOMO, which would then send Erbil a share. In the early stages of Iraqi efforts to pass a hydrocarbon law that would define the terms of the KRG's control over oil resources and the amount of revenue to which it would be entitled, Turkey supported Baghdad as a means of preventing the KRG from acquiring the economic means to pursue independence. As negotiations over the law dragged out, however, Ankara came to believe that if it wanted to access the KRG's oil, it would have to do so by engaging Erbil directly.[138]

In June 2009, the KRG began exporting 100,000 bpd to Turkey from two oilfields in the Kurdistan Region that were operated by a Norwegian firm and a Swiss Canadian company. Although revenues were provided to SOMO rather than to the KRG directly, the export deals demonstrated that Baghdad could tolerate contracts negotiated directly with Erbil, despite its position that it would refrain from working with any company that signed agreements with the KRG.[139] In May 2012, however, Erbil and Ankara reached an agreement to construct three export pipelines (one for gas and two for oil) between KRG territory and Turkey, which would enable Erbil to sell its oil to Turkey and on world markets without having to go through Baghdad.[140] In November 2013, despite Baghdad's objections, the prime ministers of Turkey and the KRG signed agreements enabling Turkey to purchase Kurdish oil and gas through new direct pipelines from the KRG to the Turkish border, with a goal of purchasing 1 million bpd of oil and

---

[138] Barkey, 2010.

[139] Kurdistan Regional Government Cabinet, 2009. See also "Kurdish Oil Exports Add Tensions to Iraq," 2009; Kane, 2010.

[140] Tocci, 2013, p. 69. See also Taşpinar and Tol, 2014.

just under 10 million cubic meters per year of natural gas by 2015 and a long-term plan to purchase 3 million bpd of oil and 19.8 million cubic meters per year of gas.[141] Prime Ministers Erdoğan and Nechirvan Barzani also signed a deal giving the state-owned Turkish oil company the right to explore 13 Kurdish fields, half of them jointly with ExxonMobil.[142] To mitigate Iraqi criticism that the KRG had no right to develop the oil resources in question, Ankara agreed that its payments would be held in a special account in Turkey, and that the KRG would receive only 17 percent of the revenues—its agreed-upon share of the Iraqi federal budget—until Baghdad and Erbil reached an agreement on revenue sharing.[143]

In December 2013, the KRG connected its regional crude oil pipeline to the existing Iraqi-Turkish export pipeline and began exports.[144] By mid-2014, Erbil was exporting only 125,000 bpd to Turkey.[145] Production steadily increased, however, in part because the KRG's seizure of the Kirkuk oilfields after ISIL's invasion gave Erbil control over a large amount of additional oil reserves. In January 2014, Turkish Energy Minister Taner Yildiz claimed that Turkey was importing 450,000 bpd from northern Iraq.[146] By late 2014, the KRG had sold approximately 30 million barrels of oil through Turkey.[147]

Both the Turkish government and Turkish companies have had to weigh potential gains from buying KRG oil against the potential costs of losing access to oil from southern Iraq—controlled by Baghdad.

---

[141] Ottaway and Ottaway, 2014.

[142] Zangeneh, 2013.

[143] Ottaway and Ottaway, 2014; Zangeneh, 2013; Tol, 2014b.

[144] Bonfield, 2014.

[145] Sheppard, 2014.

[146] "Kuzey Irak'tan Ham Petrol Akışı Yükseldi," 2015.

[147] Despite increasing oil sales through Turkey, Baghdad's continued insistence that KRG exports were illegitimate scared some purchasers off, leading to awkward situations in which cargo ships carrying Kurdish crude were prevented from docking and offloading. With onward markets cut off, Turkey began stockpiling Kurdish oil. By late 2014, the KRG had earned only $2 billion from its exports—less than it needed to cover operating costs (Natali, 2014).

Before the November 2013 deals signed by Prime Ministers Erdoğan and Barzani, the Iraqi government threatened to curtail bilateral relations with Turkey if it signed energy deals with Erbil—a warning that evidently went unheeded.[148] Baghdad may have had greater leverage over individual Turkish companies, which could presumably be replaced more easily than a neighboring sovereign state. The *Financial Times* wrote in June 2014 that "Mustafa Koç, chairman of Koç Holding, Turkey's biggest company, which owns Turkey's only refinery, said his group was under 'intense pressure' from both Ankara and the KRG to buy Kurdish oil, but that it could not do so at present without jeopardizing existing purchases from Baghdad."[149]

Turkey nevertheless has tried to maintain good relations with Baghdad even as it purchased increasing amounts of oil and gas from Erbil. According to Gareth Jenkins, just days after signing a series of energy agreements with the KRG,

> [Turkish Energy Minister Taner] Yıldız flew to Baghdad to meet with [Iraqi Deputy Prime Minister for Energy Hussain] al-Sharistani. Yıldız later told Turkish journalists . . . that Ankara respected Iraq's territorial integrity and would not allow the export of oil from the KRG without Baghdad's consent. Yıldız then flew on to an energy conference in the KRG capital of Erbil where he declared that Turkey's energy needs meant that it could not stand idly by when there were substantial reserves of Kurdish oil and natural gas so close to its border.[150]

Baghdad's own dependence on oil revenues may limit its ability to pressure Turkey to cease developing energy ties to Erbil. Moreover, Iraqi Prime Minister Abadi may be more willing to work with Turkey on oil exports than his predecessor. During a December 2014 visit to Ankara, Abadi stated that the Iraqi government supports oil exports

---

[148] Jenkins, 2013.

[149] Dombey, 2014.

[150] Jenkins, 2013.

through the Kurdish-built pipeline to Turkey, saying that such sales are "in the interest of Iraq."[151]

Ultimately, although Turkey would like to preserve its access to energy resources from both northern and southern Iraq, it has clear strategic, economic, and commercial interests in developing Kurdish oil and gas to the greatest extent possible. In the event of a political split between Baghdad and Erbil, securing continued access to the KRG's oil and gas would be a top priority for Turkey that would likely lead it to support Kurdish independence.

Military Support

Turkey's fast-growing economic interests in Iraqi Kurdistan, combined with the presence of thousands of its citizens in the Kurdistan Region, give it a strong impetus to guarantee security and stability in the KRG.[152] Although Turkey had long refrained from providing military assistance to KRG, ISIL's capture of wide swaths of Iraqi territory led Turkey to reconsider. During his first visit to Erbil as Turkish prime minister, Ahmet Davutoğlu told the press on November 21, 2014, "Iraq's security is crucial for Turkey, while the security of the Kurdish Region is the top priority issue for us. This is an issue that is directly related to Turkey's security. . . . Turkey will provide all necessary support for the security of the Kurdish region."[153] The previous month, Turkish Army special forces began training several hundred KRG peshmerga in northern Iraq as part of an effort, coordinated with the United States, to train anti-ISIL forces.[154]

Perhaps reflecting a long history of fighting Kurds rather than working with them, the Turkish military leadership vehemently opposed working with the KRG. When Ankara's political leadership

---

[151] Quoted in "Turkey, Iraq Pledge More Military Cooperation in Fight Against Islamic State," 2014.

[152] Qadir, 2015.

[153] Quoted in "Press Conference by Turkish Prime Minister Ahmet Davutoğlu and KRG President Masoud Barzani," 2014.

[154] "After Training Peshmerga, Turkey Now Set to Train and Equip FSA with US," 2014; Erkuş, 2014b; Bekdil, 2014.

decided to allow Iraqi peshmerga to pass through Turkey en route to Syria in late October 2014, senior Turkish military leaders opposed the decision. Indeed, the Turkish military did not facilitate the Kurdish fighters' presence; the peshmerga were transported on a charter plane rather than a Turkish military plane, and their transport to the Syrian border was handled by Turkey's police and intelligence services.[155]

Several countries in addition to Turkey provided the KRG with military aid in mid-2014 to bolster the Kurds' ability to withstand the ISIL onslaught. After years of receiving military aid only after it was funneled through the federal Ministry of Defense, the crisis gave Erbil the opportunity to establish its own foreign defense relations—not something it will likely want to give up or hand over to Baghdad if and when the threat from ISIL has passed.[156] Whether or not the security assistance provided by Turkey and several European countries has empowered the KRG to use force to assert its independence, the provision of direct military aid to Erbil represented an important symbolic step toward Kurdish sovereignty.

Turkey's Reaction to Various Scenarios

Turkey's reaction to Kurdish independence will be shaped by a range of domestic and regional dynamics. Turkey is likely to continue providing funding and assistance to Kurdish peshmerga in order to keep order on the Kurdish side of Turkey's border. Furthermore, to keep Syrian Kurdish groups weak, Ankara will encourage the KRG to make the PYD dependent on its largesse, which argues for further security cooperation between Ankara and Erbil.

Ankara has also built strong political, economic, and commercial ties to Erbil, particularly by purchasing Kurdish oil and encouraging Turkish companies to invest in the KRG, and it will seek to strengthen these relationships over time—particularly if Iraq continues to experience instability. Turkey has retreated from its previous concerns

---

[155] Idiz, 2014.

[156] Tanchum, 2015a.

about Kurdish independence—most notably, its demand that Kirkuk remain outside Kurdish hands and that the rights of ethnic Turkmen be protected; indeed, it has seemingly acquiesced to the KRG's governance of Kirkuk and virtually abandoned Turkmen who were fleeing ISIL attacks and distressed by Kurdish territorial seizures. As a result, Turkey is closer to supporting Kurdish independence than ever before.

Although Turkey is therefore likely to support the KRG's eventual emergence as an independent state, the means by which the KRG pursues sovereignty could affect Turkey's reaction and the degree of its support. Ankara is eager to promote stability in southern and central Iraq and to maintain ties to Baghdad (as long as it doesn't collapse into chaos), so it will be wary of Kurdish actions that earn the central government's ire. Similarly, Turkey will want an independent Kurdistan's legal claims to its oil to be as free and clear as possible so as to eliminate obstacles to large-scale oil and gas development and facilitate Turkey's purchase of Kurdish hydrocarbons. Thus, a bitter and contested divorce between Baghdad and Erbil that leads to conflict over oil rights could cause tensions between Ankara and Erbil.

Below are descriptions of Turkey's possible reactions to several likely scenarios in which the KRG pursues independence.

Unilateral Declaration of Independence

Despite Turkey's increasingly close relations with the KRG, it has not endorsed Kurdish independence. In fact, Ankara's formal position is support for the territorial integrity of Iraq, both to prevent further instability and to ensure its continued access to oil and gas resources controlled by Baghdad. In late June 2014, a senior Turkish official asserted that "the integrity of Iraq is very important to Turkey," adding, "Turkey's position is for the territorial integrity and political unity of Iraq, that's it. [We] are not in favor of any independence, that would be detrimental to that unity."[157] This fence-straddling approach—actively engage the KRG while expressing support for Baghdad's authority—

---

[157] Quoted in "Turkey Rejects Independent Kurdish State, Wants Iraq Unity Government," 2014.

has enabled Ankara to reap the benefits of close relations with the Kurds without alienating Baghdad.

If the KRG abruptly declares independence, however, Turkey would no longer be able to have it both ways. Although the Baghdad-controlled portions of the Iraq-Turkey oil pipelines stopped operating in 2014, when ISIL captured territory through which the pipeline passed, the recapture of this territory could enable the resumption of Baghdad-controlled oil to Turkey overland. An endorsement of Kurdish independence could drive Baghdad to prevent the export of oil under its control to Turkey if and when the pipeline reopens. Thus, despite Turkey's desire to maintain close ties to the new KRG, Ankara might be inclined to temper its initial support, and it may seek a way to provide practical support to the KRG—continued military assistance, continued private investment, etc.—without providing formal diplomatic recognition of its secession. Because of the costs Ankara might incur for recognizing Erbil's independence, Turkey may demand that the KRG make concessions before providing recognition. Ankara may demand more favorable oil sales terms or try to extract from Erbil a commitment to keep the PKK and PYD from establishing safe havens in its territory. Turkey's diplomatic recognition—particularly given the potential costs of alienating Baghdad—will not come free.

Erbil's unilateral declaration of independence would upset a range of carefully negotiated agreements on ownership and management of Kurdish oil exports, as Baghdad would be likely to repudiate them. Turkey would thus have to proceed carefully and slowly in its desire to purchase Kurdish crude; it may not buy as much Kurdish oil as the Kurds would like, at least for a while, and it is likely to encourage Erbil and Baghdad to reach a new hydrocarbons agreement, perhaps even offering to serve as a mediator. Disruption of the KRG's oil exports as a result of Erbil's secession could cause a severe shock to the Kurdish economy.

A sudden Erbil declaration of independence could put pressure on Turkey to intervene to protect Turkmen rights. Given Turkey's recent disinterest in Iraqi Turkmen's well-being, however, it would not likely do much on their behalf other than to demand—perhaps as a condition for earning Turkish diplomatic recognition—that the KRG provide formal political protections or rights for ethnic Turkmen.

Gradual Estrangement

Over time, in this scenario the KRG would gradually institutionalize its control over oil and territory. It would have established control over governance of disputed territories, continued oil drilling, found a pool of buyers for oil exports despite ongoing disputes with Baghdad, and figured out ways to operate the KRG government administration without receiving revenue sharing from Baghdad (possibly with infusions of Turkish aid and loans). Turkey would likely have been an active participant in the KRG's gradual accumulation of authority by pledging foreign aid, encouraging private investment, and building and/or financing energy infrastructure to import, store, and sell Kurdish oil (and gas). Ankara would have acquiesced to Kurdish control over Kirkuk and other disputed territories and accepted the status of ethnic Turkmen in the KRG polity. In exchange for ongoing and extensive political and economic support from Turkey, the KRG would likely have decided to prevent the PKK from undertaking activities on its soil and to do what it could to keep the PYD relatively weak but able to protect Syrian Kurds from abuses by ISIL or the Assad regime.

Such a slow build-up to independence would be no surprise to Turkey, which would have established such extensive bilateral ties to the KRG—and such widespread political and economic influence in it—that diplomatic recognition would no longer be a significant step. Turkish diplomatic recognition would thus formalize a broad range of political and economic ties and further enhance its influence in a new sovereign Kurdish state.

The slow, steady accumulation of political support, economic ties, and commercial investment from Turkey would strengthen the KRG's ability to move smoothly from a semi-autonomous region of Iraq to an independent, sovereign state. With Turkey firmly in the KRG's corner, other countries would be likely to extend diplomatic recognition as well. A slow progression toward independence would likely strengthen a sovereign Kurdistan's economic position as well; over time, the KRG will have developed the energy infrastructure needed to export its oil and gas, and IOCs will have had time to develop oil and gas fields, connect to pipelines, and successfully sell Kurdish hydrocarbons. Firms from Turkey and other countries will have established extensive business operations throughout the KRG, including in disputed territories. Once these economic activities become well established, Turkey, IOCs' home countries, and countries that purchase KRG-origin oil will have vested interests in ensuring that they are not undermined by a political/legal dispute between Erbil and Baghdad that had already been long settled on the ground.

Last Man Standing

If Iraq falls apart, Turkey is likely to provide vociferous support and quick diplomatic recognition to the KRG as a means of containing the chaos to south/central Iraq, bolstering stability in the north, securing Kurdish energy infrastructure, and protecting its own access to oil resources. Indeed, AKP spokesperson Huseyin Çelik indicated that Turkey would not oppose KRG independence if Iraq collapses. If Iraq breaks down, Çelik told the Kurdish newspaper *Rudaw* in mid-June 2014, "the Kurds, like any other nation, will have the right to decide their fate. . . . The Kurds of Iraq can decide for themselves the name and type of the entity they are living in."[158] Çelik echoed these sentiments in an interview with the *Financial Times* two weeks later, claiming, "In the past an independent Kurdish state was a reason for war [for Turkey] but no one has the right to say this now. . . . If Iraq is divided—and it is inevitable—they are our brothers. . . . Unfortunately, the situation in Iraq is not good, and it looks like it is going to be divided."[159]

If the central government collapses and civil war emerges, Turkey will likely take a number of steps to insulate the KRG from the unrest and protect its interests in northern Iraq. In addition to providing swift diplomatic recognition, Ankara would likely express support for Erbil's governance of Kirkuk and other disputed territories. Such a declaration would enhance the legitimacy of Kurdish governance over oil-rich

---

[158] Quoted in "Turkey's AKP Spokesman: Iraq's Kurds Have Right to Decide Their Future," 2014.

[159] Quoted in Dombey, 2014.

areas whose resources would be critical to an independent Kurdistan's economic viability, but also to insulate these energy-rich areas from the chaos of civil war in the south and thereby preserve Turkish access to the Kurdistan Region's hydrocarbons. Turkey would likely declare that it will purchase Kurdish oil and gas directly, without going through Baghdad, both as a show of support to Erbil and also to make clear to IOCs that they will still find an export market despite the conflict. Baghdad would likely be too preoccupied by violence and unrest to prevent Kurdish direct exports, and the protests of a dying state apparatus could be easily ignored by governments and oil companies alike.

To protect the nascent Kurdish state, Turkey might provide it with military materiel and training, as well as an explicit or implicit security guarantee. Ankara could deploy small numbers of special forces commandos to protect key government installations, oil infrastructure, or the Kurdish frontier with the rump Iraqi state. While Iraqi security forces or sectarian militias would be unable to mount an assault on the Kurdistan Region if they are preoccupied with fighting each other, a Turkish security umbrella could serve as a warning to Iran that the new Kurdish state lies principally within Ankara's sphere of influence. (Promises of Turkish military support could also be intended to warn ISIL to stay away, though it seems unlikely that the group would be deterred.)

In exchange for such political and military support, Turkey may demand that Kurdish authorities mitigate the threat to Turkey posed by Kurdish insurgents. In particular, Ankara could push the new Kurdish state to prevent the PKK from operating on its territory and keep PYD forces in Syria dependent on Erbil for carefully doled-out levels of economic, humanitarian, and military support. To mollify its domestic critics, Ankara could also demand that Erbil grant some degree of political representation, authority, and/or protection to ethnic Turkmen living in the Kurdistan Region.

Should the Iraqi state disintegrate, Kurdish leaders in Erbil would be well positioned to secure Turkey's swift and unequivocal support for independence. Turkish political endorsement, military assistance, and willingness to validate Erbil's rights to hydrocarbon resources would insulate the new state from regional unrest, help assure its economic prospects, and strengthen its claim to international legitimacy.

The Influence of Kurdish Nationalism

Although Turkey long feared that irredentist nationalism among Iraqi Kurds would encourage Turkish Kurds to secede, the Turkish government has appeared willing to use Iraqi Kurds as a conduit for influencing Kurds in Syria and eastern Turkey. Ankara might therefore encourage its Iraqi Kurdish allies to exercise leadership over other Kurdish groups by placing political pressure on Turkish Kurds, as it would like to see limits placed on Kurdish insurgents' ability to operate, recruit, and spread propaganda. However, it would strenuously oppose Erbil's efforts to promote any sort of pan-Kurdish nationalist sentiment that could exacerbate the Kurdish insurgency in Turkey's southeast. Despite resuming its anti-PKK campaign, Ankara would not want Iraqi Kurds to promote an irredentist pan-Kurdish identity that could lure Turkish Kurds to once again seek autonomy or secession. Turkey would likely discourage significant KRG political or military involvement in Syria, as it would not want the PYD—a PKK-aligned separatist group controlling territory along Turkey's borders—to see itself as a protector of Kurds anywhere other than inside Syria.

As a means of demonstrating that it does not support Erbil's aspirations to lead a pan-Kurdish community, Turkey could—as it had done in the past—once again vigorously advance the rights of ethnic Turkmen and provide military support to Turkmen "self-defense" militias. Such steps—which could serve as a significant internal irritant to Kurdish leaders' ability to institutionalize a firm grip on power—would demonstrate Ankara's willingness to support an independent democratic state in northern Iraq, but not an ethnic Kurdish homeland.

If Iraqi Kurdish leaders were to assert a nationalistic claim to represent Kurds throughout Iraq and the Levant, they would lose a significant amount of Turkish support for their state-building endeavor. Furthermore, by making Kurdish nationalism the foundation of the legitimacy of their nascent state, Iraqi Kurdish leaders could drive minorities in their territory into vocal opposition, thereby undermining the new government's right to rule from the start. While an independent Kurdish state may, over time, become a concrete symbol of Kurdish nationalism, an Iraqi Kurdish claim to represent and advance the interests of all ethnic Kurds could significantly alienate Turkey, Iran, and other countries in the region and thereby undermine the new state's viability.

Conclusions

Turkey has gained immensely from its close bilateral relationship with the KRG, which advances both entities' political, economic, and security interests. While Ankara appears satisfied with the status quo and its trajectory of fostering even more robust political and economic ties in the future, Kurdish independence would generate even greater strategic benefits for Turkey. As a result, Turkey is likely to support the KRG's transition to a sovereign state—particularly if it pursues independence gradually (so as not to upset the existing apple cart) or if it breaks from Baghdad so as to insulate itself from increasing violence and political turmoil in central and southern Iraq. Turkey's interests in the KRG would likely lead it to recognize even an abrupt declaration of independence by Kurdish leaders, though Ankara would have to engage in delicate diplomacy to mitigate Baghdad's resentment and prevent Turkish firms' exclusion from the Iraqi market.

To date, Turkey has reaped a range of benefits from a decade of increasingly close ties to the Kurdistan Region. Oil imports, trade, and investment by Turkish companies contribute to the Turkish economy, in large part by increasing the supplies of energy needed to fuel its rapid economic growth; make Turkey more energy independent by diversifying its supplies of oil and gas; and increase Erbil's economic dependence on Ankara. Turkey's economic importance to the KRG in turn increases its political influence, which enables it to pressure Erbil to prevent PKK activities on its soil, to undermine the dominance of PKK-aligned Kurdish groups in Syria by supporting other Syrian Kurds, and to refrain from promoting Kurdish nationalist sentiment that could upset Turkey's domestic Kurdish peace process. Turkish security assistance to the Kurdish peshmerga has enhanced the KRG's ability to keep ISIL at bay, thereby enhancing stability and security in its territory and perhaps encouraging ISIL to seek territory and targets farther afield from the Turkish border.

An independent Kurdish state may enable Turkey to advance its interests in ways that are not possible—or are at least more complicated—under the status quo. Currently, Turkey's ability to develop energy infrastructure in the KRG, sign oil contracts with Erbil, and provide military assistance to the peshmerga are complicated by the need to assuage Baghdad's concerns that such steps will deprive the federal government of income, undermine its claim to energy resources, and promote the breakup of the country. Since Turkey wants to remain on relatively good terms with Baghdad as well—particularly so Turkish companies can continue to engage in oil development deals in the southern part of the country—Ankara cannot be as proactive as it might otherwise like to be in its relations with Erbil. Moreover, other countries that seek to maintain Iraq's territorial integrity—most notably the United States—pressure Turkey to refrain from taking steps that promote or facilitate Kurdish separatism.

If the KRG became an independent sovereign state, it would largely be able to resist such pressures and to project its power more effectively. Turkey would no longer have to moderate its activities in the KRG out of fear that they would inspire retaliation from Iraq, as the KRG would already have broken from Baghdad. A sovereign Kurdistan would presumably develop close direct relations with the United States and a range of other countries, thereby enabling Turkey to enhance its ties with a neighboring state without drawing international condemnation. After Kurdish independence, Erbil and Baghdad would no longer be squabbling over revenue sharing or ownership of hydrocarbon resources. Kurdistan, as a sovereign state, would be able to claim firm ownership of the resources lying under its sovereign territory, and it would be able to develop them and sign export contracts without interference from Baghdad. (Independence may even give Erbil the upper hand in its energy diplomacy with Baghdad; instead of arguing about revenue sharing, an independent Kurdistan could conceivably charge transit fees for Iraqi oil and gas exports that pass through pipelines on Kurdish territory.) The even stronger ties that could exist between Turkey and an independent Kurdistan would enhance Ankara's political influence in Erbil while generating significant economic returns.

Greater political influence would strengthen Turkey's ability to make demands on Erbil that serve its domestic and security interests. Turkey could press an independent Kurdistan more aggressively to rein in the PKK and marginalize the Syrian PYD. Turkey could provide more comprehensive military training and materiel to Kurdish peshmerga for the purposes of fighting ISIL, securing energy infrastructure, and preventing civil unrest from spilling across its new international border with Iraq—all without having to worry about reactions from Baghdad, Washington, and other governments concerned that direct military aid to the Kurds could contribute to Iraq's fragmentation. If necessary (and if requested to do so by Erbil), Turkey could even deploy troops to an independent Kurdistan to provide military training or to bolster the country's defenses against ISIL—steps it could not take as long as the KRG remains part of Iraq; the Iraqi government—dominated by Shi'a and influenced heavily by Tehran—would not invite Sunni Turkish troops to enter Iraqi soil.

By becoming the most significant partner of an independent Kurdistan, Ankara would also be better positioned to push back against Iran's efforts to make economic and political inroads in the Kurdistan Region. By breaking from Baghdad, Erbil will have already freed itself from interference from the Iraqi central government, which is itself influenced by Tehran. Although Iran is likely to maintain considerable connections to the eastern part of a new Kurdish state, by the time the KRG might pursue independence, Erbil will have already oriented itself firmly toward Turkey.

A shift in Ankara's policies toward Turkish Kurds, insecurity in Iraq, tensions with the Iranian-influenced government in Baghdad, and a decade of gradually increasing political and economic ties to the KRG have given Turkey a strong stake in the KRG's viability, which would be enhanced by its emergence as a sovereign state. Although the means by which Erbil pursues independence may affect Turkey's near-term response, Turkey would be likely to welcome its new neighbor with open arms.

CHAPTER FIVE

Iran's Reaction to an Independent Kurdistan

The issue of an independent Kurdistan is sensitive for the Islamic Republic of Iran, as it fears unrest among its own large population of disenfranchised Kurds. Iran has a history of tensions between its ethnic minorities and the state, and with outside powers specifically attempting to use the Kurds as leverage against Tehran.

Iranian officials reacted harshly to President Barzani's July 2014 call for a referendum on Kurdish independence. Implicitly criticizing Barzani, Iran's Deputy Foreign Minister for Middle East and African Affairs Hossein Amir-Abdollahian said, "Iran has confidence that, among the Kurdish leaders, there are also wise individuals who will not allow Iraq to be broken up."[1] Furthermore, the hardline Mashregh News reported that when KRG Prime Minister Nechirvan Barzani visited Tehran in order to soften Iran's stance on potential independence, officials there warned him that the Kurds should "put an end to their maximalist demands, and ready themselves for a new situation following the end of Iraq's security crisis."[2] President Hassan Rouhani later reiterated that "all the people and leaders of Iran want the preservation of a single, united Iraq."[3]

---

[1] Quoted in "Hoshdar-e Amir-Abdollahian beh Saraan-e Kurdistan-e Aragh [Amir-Abdol-lahian's Warning to Leaders of Iraqi Kurdistan]," 2014.

[2] Quoted in "Ellat-e Hemayat-e Ankara Az Esteghlaal-e Aghlim-e Kurdistan Chiist? [What Are Reasons Behind Turkey's Support for Kurdistan's Independence?]," 2014.

[3] "Doktor Rouhani: Khaast-e Iran Hefz-e Yekparchegi va Vahdat-e Aragh Ast [Dr. Rouhani: Iran's Desire Is Preservation of Single, United Iraq]," undated.

However, although leaders in Tehran strongly prefer that Iraq's Kurds do not declare independence, their reaction to such an event would be tempered by economic interests as well as the desire to prevent Iran's rivals—namely Turkey, the United States, and Israel—from having free rein in a new country sharing a border with Iran. If Kurdish independence were to occur, the best scenario for Iran would be one in which Erbil made the decision following drawn-out discussions with Baghdad, which would provide time and the political environment for the Iranians to adopt a pragmatic policy that could adjust to a new neighboring state as well as manage the expectations of its own Kurdish population. On the other hand, if Erbil's declaration were abrupt, perhaps prompted by a sudden flare-up with the Baghdad government or disintegration of the Iraqi state, Iran's threat perception would be heightened, allowing security hawks to take the lead in determining Tehran's Kurdish policy; Iran likely would deal with its own Kurds solely through security measures, and Kurdish Iranian dissident groups based in Iraq could respond by intensifying militant activities against Islamic Republic targets. Moreover, an independent Kurdistan that does not espouse a pan-Kurdish ideology that could invigorate Iranian Kurds to seek autonomy would also be more acceptable to Iran. If the new Kurdistan government did claim the pan-Kurdish mantle, Iran may decide to cut economic ties with the new state or attempt to destabilize it, even though doing so would cede influence over Erbil to its geopolitical rivals.

In any scenario, the Islamic Republic's *perception* of how its own Kurds would react to an independent Kurdistan on its border is likely to influence its overall strategy more so than the actual Kurdish Iranian response. In other words, even if the majority of Iran's Kurds did not see the new state as a model to follow, Tehran would view its existence as a latent source of inspiration. Iranian Kurdish activism, thereafter, could be seen as an attempt to undermine the Islamic Republic. However, the manner in which Erbil declares independence is important in that it would color Tehran's assessment of how capable Iranian Kurdish activists would be to threaten its grip on power. The more abrupt or aggressive Erbil's declaration of independence, the more harshly Iran would crack down on its own Kurds—in turn intensifying Kurdish nationalism in the country. Ultimately, in treating its Kurdish population as a security threat, Iran could bring about the very conditions it seeks to prevent.

Iran's Kurds

The Islamic Republic's reaction to an independent Kurdish state will be influenced by relations with its own Kurdish population as well as its perception regarding the intentions of outside powers. The Persian-majority state has had tense relations with the Kurds in its territory since at least the 16th century, when the Safavid shahs attempted to exert greater control over the empire's tribes.[4] During the 20th century, both the Soviet Union and Iraq used Iranian Kurds as a means of attaining regional dominance.

Approximately 7 to 9 million Kurds live in Iran, comprising a little less than 40 percent of the Middle East's overall Kurdish population.[5] As the second-largest ethnic minority group in Iran (after Turkish Azeris), Kurds mostly populate the contiguous Iranian provinces of Kurdistan, West Azerbaijan, Kermanshah, and Ilam—a combined area that Kurdish nationalists refer to as Rojhelat.[6] Another 1.5 million Kurds, known as the Khorasani Kurds, live in northeastern Iran.[7] Forcibly resettled in the area in the 17th century by Safavid rulers, the Khorasani Kurds generally do not interact with the broader Kurdish community. Kurds living in northern Iran share the Kurmanji Kurdish dialect with Kurds in southeast Turkey, northern Iraq, and northern Syria. In the southern parts of Iran's Kurdish region, Kurds speak both Sorani—the dialect of Iraq's Talabani clan—and Gorani, which is also spoken in Iraq's Halabja region.

---

[4] Yildiz and Taysi, 2007.

[5] Yildiz and Taysi, 2007.

[6] Van Wilgenburg, 2014.

[7] "Iranian Kurdistan," 2010.

Pre-Revolutionary Period

For much of the first half of the 20th century, the Iranian city of Mahabad was home to the intellectual leaders of Kurdish nationalism, and the center of resistance against the state.[8] When he rose to the throne in 1925, Reza Pahlavi set out to tame the country's tribal communities, which included the Kurds. Following Turkish President Ataturk's lead, Reza Shah also attempted to do away with ethnic and religious diversity and to make everyone "Iranian," banning textbooks and radio broadcasts in non-Persian languages.[9]

In January 1946, shortly after the occupying Allied forces deposed Reza Shah, Iran's Kurds declared an independent Republic of Kurdistan, with its capital in Mahabad. Masoud Barzani's father, Mullah Mustafa Barzani, was appointed defense minister.[10] However, riven by internal tribal conflicts, and receiving little but moral support from the Soviet Union, the republic fell to Mohammad Reza Shah's troops in December 1946.[11] Although it lasted for only one year, the Mahabad republic holds an important place in Kurds' national memory as the only independent Kurdish state in history.

Iran's Kurds maintained a rocky relationship with the state for the remainder of the Pahlavi monarchy. In the 1950s, the Kurdish Democratic Party of Iran (KDPI) supported Mohammad Mossadegh and, in 1968, a group of Baghdad-backed KDPI members began an insurgency against the Iranian government from a base in Iraq. This was two years after Mohammad Reza Pahlavi had begun backing the Iraqi KDP in its struggle against the Baghdad government. To maintain the Shah's support, and in one of repeated instances in which Kurdish groups have worked against their ethnic brethren on behalf of outside state sponsors, KDP leader Masoud Barzani's men killed numerous KDPI fighters in Iraq.[12] Following the 1975 signing of the Algiers

---

[8] Ahmadzadeh and Stansfield, 2010.

[9] Tohidi, 2009.

[10] Namazi, 2014.

[11] Yildiz and Taysi, 2007.

[12] Bruinessen, 1986.

Accord, Tehran and Baghdad refrained from using Kurdish proxies for several years.[13]

The Revolutionary Period

After decades of clashes with the Pahlavi monarchy, Iranian Kurds supported the Islamic Revolution, which overthrew the Shah. KDPI leaders returned from exile to Mahabad carrying with them hopes of greater Kurdish rights in a new political system.

However, following in his predecessors' footsteps, Ayatollah Khomeini balked at empowering Iran's minority communities out of fear that they would be exploited by the country's enemies.[14] Rejecting the KDPI's request for regional autonomy over social and cultural affairs, Khomeini declared jihad against the Kurds in August 1979.[15] Throughout the 1980s, tens of thousands were killed in the ensuing fighting between Kurdish insurgents and the newly formed Islamic Revolutionary Guards Corps (IRGC).[16] Moreover, with the Iran-Iraq war raging, Tehran and Baghdad once again turned to Kurdish proxies. Baghdad reverted to aiding the KDPI, while Iran focused most of its support on the PUK in Iraq.

Iran's Kurdish opposition faced other setbacks in the late 1980s and early 1990s. The establishment of the KRG in 1991 benefited Tehran, as the autonomous region's authorities clamped down on Iranian Kurdish attacks coming from northern Iraq.[17] The period also saw a spate of Tehran-sponsored assassinations, including the 1989 killing of KDPI leader Abd al-Rahman Qasimlu in Vienna.[18] Qasimlu's suc-

---

[13] In 1975, Iran and Iraq signed the Algiers Accord, which was meant to settle their dispute over border regions—including the Shatt al-Arab waterway—and to bring an end to the Kurdish insurgencies. In 1980, Saddam Hussein abolished the agreement and invaded Iran.

[14] This was despite early indications by revolutionary leaders that the Kurds would be granted autonomy within the new republic.

[15] Ahmadzadeh and Stansfield, 2010.

[16] Bozorgmehr, 2014a.

[17] Ahmadzadeh and Stansfield, 2010.

[18] Ahmadzadeh and Stansfield, 2010.

cessor, Sadiq Sharafkandi, was assassinated in Berlin in 1992.[19] During this time, the Islamic Republic is thought to have assassinated more than 200 Iranian Kurds living in Iraqi Kurdistan.[20]

The reformist era ushered in by President Mohammad Khatami (1997–2005) led to improvements in the lives of Iran's Kurds. Journals in the Kurdish language, which first sprouted during the latter part of the Ali Akbar Hashemi-Rafsanjani administration (1989–1997), proliferated under Khatami, as did Kurdish cultural and literary societies.[21] Kurdish youths attended universities in increasing numbers and became politically active. Khatami also appointed Kurds to his cabinet and appointed Kurdistan province's first Kurdish governor, Abdollah Ramazanzade.[22] However, like many other reformists, Kurds had become disillusioned by Khatami's second term, as the president struggled to push back against his hardline opponents. In 2005, increased tensions led to six weeks of riots in Mahabad, which erupted after security forces assassinated Kurdish activist Shivan Qaderi.[23]

The brief freedoms that Kurds had enjoyed came to an end when Mahmoud Ahmadinejad became president (2005–2013). Under his presidency, Kurdish newspapers were once again banned, and an increased number of activists were arrested. Despite initial optimism following President Hassan Rouhani's election in 2013, human rights activists have been disappointed by his inability to stop repression against minorities. One dissident organization, the Democratic Party of Iranian Kurdistan, claims that between March 2014 and March 2015, Iran arrested 956 Kurds.[24] During the same period, security forces reportedly shot 153 Kurds, 57 of whom died.[25] Kurdish activists

---

[19] Natali, 2005.

[20] Ahmadzadeh and Stansfield, 2010.

[21] Tohidi, 2009.

[22] Yildiz and Taysi, 2007.

[23] "Iranian Kurdistan," 2010.

[24] Democratic Party of Iranian Kurdistan, 2015a.

[25] Democratic Party of Iranian Kurdistan, 2015a.

also expressed concern that, following the signing of a nuclear deal, the West would ignore Iranian human rights abuses.[26]

Communal Dynamics

While Iranian Kurds would welcome the emergence of an independent Kurdistan in northern Iraq, the extent of the connection they felt to it likely would vary, depending on multiple factors ranging from tribal, linguistic, and religious affiliation to geographic location within Iran to political ideology.

Iranian Kurds are not a monolithic group. Communities are organized differently according to region. Among the Kurds in the Zagros range, tribal affiliations tend to be strongest, borne out of their pastoralist and herding lifestyle.[27] Kurds in the plains live in agricultural villages. In urban areas of Iran's Kurdish region, Kurds commonly work as teachers, traders, or shopkeepers. In these environments, Kurdish tribal connections tend to be weaker. Dialect varies by region, with Kurds in northern Iran speaking the Kurmanji dialect and southern Kurds speaking Sorani and Gurani. There is some religious diversity among the Kurds. Although most are Sunni, a sizable Kurdish Shi'a population is centered in Kermanshah, while Kurdish Yazidis and followers of the Ahl-e Haqq faith also live in Iran.[28]

Based on interviews conducted inside Iran in 2013 by the Ankara-based International Middle East Peace Research Center, the connection that Iranian Kurds feel with other Kurds is influenced by one's location inside Iran.[29] For instance, Kurds living north of the West Azerbaijan provincial capital of Orumieh tend to be well informed of the situation that Kurds face in Turkey. Residents of Sanandaj and Kermanshah, on the other hand, lack substantive knowledge of the issue. Conversely,

---

[26] Zaman, 2015b.

[27] Yildiz and Taysi, 2007.

[28] Yazidism is a pre-Islamic religion with origins in Mesopotamia. The Ahl-e Haqq faith, also referred to as Yarsanism, is a mystical form of Islam followed mostly by Gurani-speaking Kurds in Iran, Iraq, and Turkey. While Ahl-e Haqq revere Ali as a divine figure, most followers of the faith do not consider themselves to be Shi'a (Mir-Hosseini, 1994, p. 267).

[29] International Middle East Peace Research Center, 2014.

the survey found that Iranian Kurds south of Orumieh have closer relations with Iraqi Kurds than do residents of Iran's northern region. The weak political connection between Iran's Kurds and their brethren in neighboring countries was illustrated in June 2015, following the Kurds' historic victory in Turkey's parliamentary elections. While a small handful of Kurdish youths gathered in the streets of the West Azerbaijan towns of Mahabad and Bukan, there were no other reports of public celebrations in any other parts of Iranian Kurdistan.[30]

The reaction of Iranian Kurds as a whole could also vary from Kurds outside of the country for cultural reasons. Analysts posit that because of similarities between Persian and Kurdish culture, Iran's Kurds tend to have more of an attachment to their country than Kurds living in Turkey, Iraq, or Syria.[31] According to Omid Varzandeh, the head of Azad University's Kurdish Studies Center, "The view that Iran [also] belongs to us is gaining strength."[32] And although an estimated 30,000 Iranian Kurds have found work in the Kurdistan Region, many look forward to returning to Iran if the economy improves.[33]

Along these lines, and despite the attention commentators often pay to Kurdish political parties and insurgents, most of the political activities in which Iran's young generation of Kurds participates are part of broader Iranian civil society activism, calling for general democracy and economic improvement rather than focusing simply on Kurdish rights.[34] In 2014, of the approximately 62 non-labor protests that occurred in Kurdish provinces, most were related to general, non-Kurdish issues, such as the poor state of the economy, environmental

---

[30] If, on the other hand, the almost total absence of celebration was the result of Kurdish Iranians' fear of a government crackdown (rather than lack of interest in Turkey's Kurdish politics), then one could expect the same calculation to be made regarding celebrations over Iraqi Kurdish independence, which would be an even more sensitive issue for Tehran ("Koshteh Shodan-e Javanaan-e Manaateq-e Kordneshin-e Iran Dar Fa'aliatha-ye Nezami-ye Da'esh [Youths from Iranian Kurdish Regions Killed in ISIS Military Activities]," 2015).

[31] Natali, 2005.

[32] Quoted in Bozorgmehr, 2014a.

[33] Ridha, 2015.

[34] Yildiz and Taysi, 2007.

problems, and university problems.[35] It is not surprising that economic protests are prominent among the Kurds. Both the Pahlavi monarchy and the Islamic Republic have maintained Iran's border regions in an underdeveloped state to prevent the ethnic minorities living there from gaining too much power.[36] As a minority, the Kurds have been disproportionately disadvantaged relative to broader Iranian society. As of late 2014, of the five Iranian provinces with the lowest proportion of their workforce employed in the industrial sector, three were centers of Kurdish population.[37] Moreover, Kurdistan province is 29th out of 31 Iranian provinces in level of industrial development.[38] High unemployment has led to an active black market economy, with Kurdish porters, or *kulbar*, smuggling goods from Iraq into Iran. Around 100 Kurdish *kulbar* were killed by Iranian security forces in 2012 and 2013.[39] Meanwhile, of the 24 protest events that *were* ethnically focused, 16 were rallies held in solidarity with Kurds fighting against ISIL in Syria and Iraq. However, illustrating the Iranian government's concern over any mobilization of Kurds—even those who are protesting against Iran's enemy—security forces attacked and detained many participants.[40] In April 2015, two Kurds who had been involved in pro-Kobani protests were sentenced to five months in prison and 30 lashes.[41]

This is not to say that Kurdish identity plays little role in protests. While the root cause of a protest may not be related to ethnicity, grievances borne of decades of anti-Kurdish discrimination can intensify

---

[35] Survey of official Iranian and dissident media.

[36] Yildiz and Taysi, 2007.

[37] The national average for the 2014 summer quarter was 32.9 percent. The rates for the Kurd-dominated provinces of West Azerbaijan, Kurdistan, and Ilam were 23.6 percent, 24.7 percent, and 25 percent, respectively (Statistical Center of Iran, 2014).

[38] Bozorgmehr, 2014b.

[39] Bozorgmehr, 2014b; Hawramy, 2013.

[40] "Hamle-ye Nirooha-ye Amniyati be Tajamo-e Hemaayat az Kobani Dar Marivan [Security Forces in Marivan Attack Rally in Support of Kobani]," 2014.

[41] "Do Fa'aal-e Kargari Dar Sanandaj Baraye Tajamo-e Hemayat Az Kobani beh Habs va Shalagh Mahkoum Shodand [Two Labor Activists in Sanandaj Sentenced to Prison and Lashings for Protest in Support of Kobani]," 2015.

the situation. Moreover, a large protest occurring in a Kurdish city is often followed by incidents in other Kurdish towns of Iran, where residents protest in solidarity with their ethnic brethren. In May 2015, hundreds of Kurds gathered outside of a hotel in Mahabad to protest the death of a Kurdish housekeeper who had fallen to her death from a fourth-floor balcony after allegedly trying to escape sexual assault at the hands of a security officer. Protests spread to other Kurdish cities in Iran out of solidarity with the victim; the protesters who were attacked and detained by government forces.[42]

Political Parties

Throughout most of modern Iranian history, Kurdish politics has been marked by bitter in-fighting that has prevented the Kurds from maintaining a unified front to resist the state. Even during the Kurds' struggle against the Islamic Republic in the 1980s, some Iranian Kurdish tribal leaders allied with Tehran to gain leverage over rival tribes.[43] In the event that the KRG declares independence, the Iranian government could attempt to sow discord among Iranian Kurds in order to stave off a potential push for autonomy.

The two most established Iranian Kurdish parties are the KDPI and Komala. Enemies for much of their existence, they fought a civil war that lasted from 1984 to 1988.[44] KDPI was established in 1945 and is the oldest Iranian Kurdish political party. Its traditional base, composed predominantly of urban middle-class intellectuals, is centered in the Mahabad area.[45] Although the KDPI has given up violence as its main form of resistance, it still challenges the core tenets of the Islamic Republic by calling for a secular government in addition to pursuing federal autonomy for ethnic minorities.[46] The group's fighters, however,

---

[42] "Tajamo-e Mo'tarezaan Dar Mahabad Beh Khoshoonat Keshideh Shodeh [Protest in Mahabad Turns Violent]," 2015; "E'terazaat-e Rooz-e Kozashte-ye Shahrha-ye Kordestan [Yesterday's Protests in Kurdish Cities]," 2015.

[43] Yildiz and Taysi, 2007.

[44] Ahmadzadeh and Stansfield, 2010.

[45] Yildiz and Taysi, 2007.

[46] "Iranian Kurdistan," 2010.

do clash with Iranian forces on occasion. In September 2014, KDPI peshmerga claimed that they were ambushed by security forces outside of Marivan, in Iran's Kurdistan province.[47] Komala was founded in 1969 as a radical Marxist organization and attacked the KDPI for serving the "bourgeoisie."[48] Komala's traditional base comes from the area around Sanandaj. Further illustrating the fractious nature of Kurdish politics, the party split into two groups in 2000: the communist Komalah and the less hardline socialist Komala.[49] Today, Komala calls for Iran to become a socialist federation of states.[50] Because of restrictions within Iran, KDPI and Komala leaders reside in Iraq and Europe, the latter serving as home to around 50,000 diaspora Iranian Kurds.[51] In Iraq, both groups maintain headquarters in Sulaimaniyah.[52]

Despite their historical differences, KDPI and Komala signed a memorandum of cooperation in 2012.[53] One potential reason behind the reconciliation is shared concern over their increased irrelevance among Kurds inside Iran.[54] While in the past, the parties could boast thousands of members, they now are thought to number only in the hundreds.[55] This is because many young Kurdish activists feel disconnected from the traditional political parties, preferring to engage in grassroots activism rather than top-down politics.[56] For instance, despite both parties calling for a boycott of the 2013 Iranian presiden-

---

[47] Saadullah, 2014.

[48] Bruinessen, 1986.

[49] Yildiz and Taysi, 2007.

[50] Komala Party of Iranian Kurdistan, 2001.

[51] Natali, 2005.

[52] Democratic Party of Iranian Kurdistan, undated; "Etela'ie-ye Dabirkhane-ye Hezb-e Demokraat Darbare-ye Youresh beh Kamp-e Hezb-e Demokrat [KDPI Secretariat's Announcement Regarding Attack on KDPI's Camp]," 2015.

[53] Komala Party of Iranian Kurdistan, 2013.

[54] "PKK Blocks KDPI Convoy as Inter-Kurdish Conflict Continues," 2015; Van Wilgenburg, 2014.

[55] Zaman, 2015b.

[56] Ahmadzadeh and Stansfield, 2010.

tial election, Kurds turned out to vote in large numbers. Reacting to his campaign promises to improve the situation of minorities, 72 percent of Iran's Kurds voted for Rouhani.[57] How long relations between the KDPI and Komala stay cordial remains to be seen. In September 2014, the Iranian government announced that its Ministry of Intelligence had been holding backchannel talks with each group.[58] A KDPI official at the time expressed skepticism regarding Iran's motives, citing the possibility that Tehran intends to play the parties against each other.[59]

Moreover, in the event of increased unrest in Iran's Kurdish region, the two parties could resume militant activities against Iranian forces as a means of currying local favor. For instance, in May 2015, two days after widespread protests broke out in Iran in response to a Kurdish woman's death in Mahabad, KDPI deployed its peshmerga fighters to its old bases on the Iranian border in order "to defend the Kurdish people against Iranian aggression."[60] According to Kurdish media, some of the KDPI fighters intended to head to the Iranian town of Oshnavieh (in the province of West Azerbaijan) before PKK fighters stopped them.[61] Several weeks later, the KDPI announced that it had "made a strategic decision to reinvigorate the struggle against the Islamic Republic of Iran," which would entail a "greater emphasis on the role of Peshmerga."[62] As part of this effort, the KDPI would be sending its militants into Iran to strengthen its "vast clandestine network" and to strengthen its connections with the local population. From the time that the KDPI deployed to the Iraq-Iranian border until early June 2015, 11 IRGC members were killed in clashes with Kurdish militants.[63]

---

[57] Van Wilgenburg, 2014; Bozorgmehr, 2014b.

[58] "Iran Reveals It Is Negotiating with Its Rebel Kurdish Groups," 2014.

[59] "Iran Reveals It Is Negotiating with Its Rebel Kurdish Groups," 2014.

[60] Democratic Party of Iranian Kurdistan, 2015b.

[61] "PKK Blocks KDPI Convoy as Inter-Kurdish Conflict Continues," 2015; Sadiq, 2015.

[62] Democratic Party of Iranian Kurdistan, 2015d.

[63] Although the KDPI did not claim responsibility for the attacks, the group highlighted the following correlation: Since the KDPI deployed its peshmerga forces to the border region

Kurdish Militants

The major militant Kurdish groups operating inside Iran—namely, the PJAK and the Kurdish Salafists—have non-indigenous roots, and thus do not appear to have strong backing among the public. Until recently, the political platforms of the KDPI and Komala did not focus on violence against the Iranian government (it remains to be seen to what extent the KDPI will resume violent activities following its June 2015 announcement that it would begin emphasizing the role of its peshmerga).

In recent years, the PJAK has been the main Kurdish insurgent group fighting the Iranian government. The PJAK was established in 1999 as an offshoot of the PKK. Based along the Iran-Iraq border in the Qandil Mountains, the group began its armed resistance in 2005—one year after Tehran declared the PKK a terrorist organization. By 2011, the PJAK claimed to have 3,000 fighters, half of whom were women.[64] Iran's attacks on the group have repeatedly crossed over into Iraqi territory. In 2010, for instance, Iran shelled PJAK bases in Iraqi Kurdistan for two weeks.[65] In 2011, as part of the PKK's broader rapprochement with Iran, the PJAK agreed to a ceasefire with Tehran, with some speculating at the time that PKK leader Ocalan was ultimately preparing for the possibility of resumed fighting against the Turkish state.[66] However, coinciding with the increased unrest in Iraq, clashes have resumed between the PJAK and Iran. In 2014, there were around 20 clashes between Iranian forces and Kurdish militants, resulting in the death of around 70 government agents and a dozen Kurds.[67] All but four of these incidents involved PJAK insurgents (the remaining four involved KDPI forces, who claim they were acting in self-defense after

---

between eastern (Iranian) and southern (Iraqi) Kurdistan, several IRGC members have been killed or injured in different cities and towns in eastern Kurdistan (Democratic Party of Iranian Kurdistan, 2015b, 2015e, 2015f, 2015g; "Tanesh va Na-araami dar Oshnavieh [Tensions and Unrest in Oshnavieh]," 2015).

[64] Zambelis, 2011.

[65] Richards, 2013.

[66] Van Wilgenburg, 2014.

[67] Survey of official Iranian and dissident media.

being ambushed by security forces). In February 2015, in response to Iran's execution of three Kurdish political prisoners, PJAK warned that the "Iranian state has started a dangerous process."[68] The following day, Iran shelled the group's Qandil Mountain bases.[69] Iranian fighter jets continued to bomb PJAK bases through April 2015.[70]

Despite its use of violence, PJAK does not call for Kurdish secession, but rather for regional autonomy within Iran—a demand that generally aligns with those of the KDPI and Komala. Perhaps in an attempt to gain more legitimacy among Iranian Kurds, in May 2014, PJAK announced that it was forming a new political party called the Democratic Community and a Free Rojhelat (KODAR), which would be co-led by one man and one woman.[71]

Although the Iranian government will continue to see PJAK as a security threat, the group's ties to the PKK can be of benefit to Tehran. As long as the group maintains its allegiance to a Turkish Kurdish movement, its influence among Iranian Kurds is likely to be limited. PJAK also is unlikely to support a Barzani-led independent Kurdistan that would compete for influence with the PKK. Moreover, if the PKK were to come to an agreement with the Tehran-backed Damascus regime regarding Kurdish territory in northern Syria, it could lead to a drop in PJAK activities in Iran.

While Salafi Kurds have yet to stage attacks inside Iran, they remain of concern to the Iranian government. Fighters from the Kurdish militant group Ansar al-Islam entered the country in 2003 after U.S. forces forced them out of Halabja, where Salafi extremists had been based since the 1980s.[72] By 2004, KRG officials were expressing concern that Iran was allowing the Kurdish Salafi groups to operate

---

[68] Quoted in "KCK: Iran Has Started a Dangerous Process," 2015.

[69] "Iranian Army Shells Kandil Area," 2015.

[70] Zaman, 2015b.

[71] "Iranian Kurdish Group Shifts Policy, Seeking Democratic Autonomy," 2014.

[72] Van Wilgenburg, 2015.

in Marivan and Sanandaj as a means of pressuring Erbil, which had become closer with Washington since the U.S. invasion.[73]

In 2005, Tehran cracked down on the remnants of Ansar al-Islam in the country. Some were detained, while others fled to Afghanistan.[74] However, in 2014, Salafi extremists in Iran apparently became emboldened following the success of ISIL in Iraq. By the fall of 2014, Kurdish villagers in western Iran were claiming to have seen ISIL militants conducting intelligence, surveillance, and reconnaissance missions near their villages.[75] In at least two instances in late 2014, Iranian security forces clashed with supposed ISIL fighters in the provinces of West Azerbaijan and Kurdistan.[76]

According to Iranian Kurdish media, as of April 2015, 141 residents of Saghez, located in the province of Kurdistan, had joined Salafi militants in Iraq, Syria, Afghanistan, and Pakistan.[77] Iranian towns from which specifically ISIL volunteers have come include Saghez, Kermanshah, Ravansar, Naghade, Javanrud, and Mahabad.[78] As of April 2015, more than 40 Iranian Kurds had been killed fighting alongside ISIL.[79] Also in April 2015, IRGC intelligence forces arrested around 300 Kurdish residents of Saghez, claiming that they were radical Salafis.[80] While some who were arrested did attend a Salafi mosque

---

[73] Mehdi Khalaji writes that Al-Qaeda in Iraq head Abu Musab al-Zarqawi even spent several months on the Iranian side of the border in order to mobilize Kurdish jihadis there (Khalil, 2007; Khalaji, 2014).

[74] Khalaji, 2014.

[75] Scotten, 2014.

[76] Scotten, 2014.

[77] "Hodood-e 300 Shahrvand-e Saghezi Tavasot-e Nirooha-ye Amniati Bazdaasht Shodand [Around 300 Residents of Saghez Arrested by Security Forces]," 2015.

[78] "Koshteh Shodan-e Javanaan-e Manaateq-e Kordneshin-e Iran Dar Fa'aliatha-ye Nezami-ye Da'esh [Youths from Iranian Kurdish Regions Killed in ISIS Military Activities]," 2015; "Estemraar-e Koshteh Shodan-e Javanaan-e Kord Dar Fa'aaliatha-ye Nezami-ye Da'esh [Continuation of Kurdish Youth Deaths in ISIS Operations]," 2015.

[79] "Estemraar-e Koshteh Shodan-e Javanaan-e Kord Dar Fa'aaliatha-ye Nezami-ye Da'esh [Continuation of Kurdish Youth Deaths in ISIS Operations]," 2015.

[80] "Hodood-e 300 Shahrvand-e Saghezi Tavasot-e Nirooha-ye Amniati Bazdaasht Shodand [Around 300 Residents of Saghez Arrested by Security Forces]," 2015.

in town, Kurdish activists claimed that the government was using the threat of terrorism as an excuse to round up political activists.[81]

Iran's Ties to the KRG

Although its ties to Shi'a parties in Iraq receive the most attention, Iran also cultivates close relations with Iraqi Kurds to further its own interests. In the event of an independent Kurdistan, Iran could attempt to exploit rifts among the Iraqi Kurdish parties to gain political leverage. The potential benefit to Iran of this strategy was on display in January 2014, when leaders from the KDP and PUK asked the Islamic Republic to intercede in breaking a deadlock over the formation of the KRG government.[82] Since then, Iran-KRG relations have continued to strengthen, with Ali Larijani's December 2014 trip to Iraqi Kurdistan marking the first time a Majlis speaker had visited the Kurdistan Region.[83]

The PUK is Iran's closest Kurdish partner. Since the Islamic Republic's founding, Iran has had close relations with Jalal Talabani, the PUK leader and former Iraqi president (2005–2014).[84] Beginning in 1983, Iran provided the group with weaponry to help fight Saddam Hussein. In 2008, it was President Talabani who reportedly met Quds Force Commander Qassem Soleimani at the Iranian border and pleaded with him to bring an end to fighting between Muqtada al-Sadr's forces and the Baghdad government.[85] According to leading party member Ala Talabani, when the PUK leader became ill, it was Iran's "role behind the curtains" that heavily influenced the choice for his succes-

---

[81] "Hodood-e 300 Shahrvand-e Saghezi Tavasot-e Nirooha-ye Amniati Bazdaasht Shodand [Around 300 Residents of Saghez Arrested by Security Forces]," 2015.

[82] Van Wilgenburg, 2014.

[83] Dastmali, 2015.

[84] Javedanfar, 2005.

[85] Allam, Landay, and Strobel, 2008.

sor in 2013.[86] Furthermore, some PUK leaders have openly expressed their preference for Iranian, rather than Turkish or Saudi, involvement in Iraqi affairs.[87] Because the KDP is reluctant to supply its PUK rivals with weapons, the PUK relies heavily on Iran for arms.[88] In fact, PUK peshmerga cooperated with Shi'a militias in liberating Amerli and Jalawla from ISIL control.[89] And when ISIL militants approached the Iranian border, PUK peshmerga provided Iran with intelligence that allowed the IRGC to accurately target the militants with artillery.[90] Tehran's close ties to PUK also help in countering KDPI members in Iraq. According to the KDPI, in March 2015, a PUK-run police force raided the group's Azadi Camp in the town of Koya, "severely beating the women, children and even the peshmerga."[91] This was apparently not the first time PUK forces had raided the camp. Meanwhile, according to the PKK, Iran convinced the KRG to prevent the KDPI from joining in the anti-ISIL fight.[92] Further illustrating Iran's close relations with the PUK, during his trip to Iraqi Kurdistan, Ali Larijani raised eyebrows in deciding to visit Talabani in Sulaimaniyah before going to the KRG capital of Erbil.[93]

Despite its long history of support to his PUK rivals, the Islamic Republic has also built ties with Masoud Barzani, who serves both as president of the KRG and as leader of the KDP.[94] Iran's relationship with both Kurdish parties is reflective of Tehran's overall strategy in

---

[86] Quoted in Ahmed, 2013.

[87] Richards, 2013.

[88] "Will Arming Peshmerga Tip Balance of Power in Iraq?" 2014.

[89] Mohammed Salih, 2015a; Kittleson, 2014.

[90] Parker, Dehghanpisheh, and Coles, 2015.

[91] Quoted in "Etela'ie-ye Dabirkhane-ye Hezb-e Demokraat Darbare-ye Youresh beh Kamp-e Hezb-e Demokrat [KDPI Secretariat's Announcement Regarding Attack on KDPI's Camp]," 2015.

[92] Because the KDPI is located in PUK-controlled territory, it is likely that the PKK was referring to the PUK as the authorities who stopped the KDPI from entering the fight ("Iran Has Terrorized the Kurds Alliance," 2014).

[93] Dastmali, 2015.

[94] Brennan et al., 2013.

Iraq: gaining influence with multiple actors with the intent not only of playing one rival against another, but to also become indispensable as a power broker and mediator of disputes.[95] An improvement in ties with Iran is also to Barzani's benefit. In early 2015, a source close to the KDP said that the party was trying to foster closer relations with Tehran partly in the hope that "Iran will back away from the PUK and PKK."[96] Furthermore, Iranian military support has been essential in the fight against ISIL. In August 2014, Barzani thanked Iran for being "the first state to help us" in the fight against ISIL.[97] The KDP may also see Iran's provision of arms to the PUK as beneficial in that it allows the KDP to keep the superior Western arms for itself. Although most analysts see the KDP as closer to Turkey than to Iran, Barzani claims that the KRG is trying to maintain balance in its relations between the two countries.[98] However, a potential future struggle between peshmerga and Shi'a militias over disputed territories, such as Kirkuk, could sour Barzani's perception of Iran.[99]

Economic Relations

The KRG's economic development has benefited Iran and strengthened Tehran's relations with Erbil. While in 2000, official annual trade between Iran and Iraqi Kurdistan stood at $100 million, it had reached $6 billion by 2015.[100] In 2012, representatives of more than 100 Iranian companies visited Iraqi Kurdistan as part of the new Iranian-Kurdistan Region Economic Forum.[101] By the next year, the KRG was trucking around 30,000 bpd of crude oil to Iran's Bandar Imam Kho-

---

[95] Nader, 2015.

[96] Hemin Salih, 2015a.

[97] "Barzani: Iran Gave Weapons to Iraq's Kurds," 2014.

[98] "Massoud Barzani: Hich Rokhdaadi Maane'ye Esteghlaal-e Kurdistan as Aragh Nemishavad [Massoud Barzani: Nothing Will Get in the Way of Kurdistan's Independence from Iraq]," 2015.

[99] Salama and Janssen, 2015.

[100] Richards, 2013; "Iran-Iraqi Kurdistan Region Annual Trade Hits $6bn," 2015.

[101] Richards, 2013.

meini port, from where it was shipped to international markets.[102] In April 2014, Tehran and Erbil signed an agreement to build oil and gas pipelines from the Kurdish region to Iran.[103] In February 2015, Iranian and Kurdish officials discussed building a rail link between the Iranian city of Kermanshah and Sulaimaniyah.[104] And in March 2015, the KRG announced that it was negotiating to have Iran refine Kurdish oil and send it back to Kurdistan for internal use. It would also be buying Iranian gas for household use and power stations.[105] That Iran has conducted these activities despite Baghdad's strong objections—namely, that it could further embolden the Kurds to move toward independence—indicates that financial benefits may temper Iranian concerns on the issue of Kurdish independence.[106]

In addition to official trade, there is an enormous black market economy, which has helped Iran bypass banking sanctions. Each year, billions of dollars in goods are smuggled into Iran from the Kurdish region, including home appliances and electronics.[107] While some businessmen (and corrupt security forces who guard the border) profit from the trade, most Iranian Kurds do not.[108]

Limits to Iranian Influence

Despite efforts to strengthen ties, Iran and the KRG have disagreed over issues of Persian chauvinism. For instance, in May 2014, the KRG Department of Foreign Relations summoned the Iranian consul general in Erbil to protest an article on the consular website that referred to Iran as the "true great home and motherland" of the Kurds and called

---

[102] "Iraqi Kurdistan Opens Official Crude Oil Trade Route via Iran," 2013.

[103] Tanchum, 2015a.

[104] "Iran, Iraq Kurdistan Region to Expand Cooperation," 2015.

[105] "Kurdistan Negotiating Gas and Oil Deals with Iran," 2015.

[106] Tanchum, 2015a.

[107] Bozorgmehr, 2014b.

[108] Bozorgmehr, 2014b.

the Kurdish language a "dialect" of Persian.[109] The article also advised against Kurdish independence. In another instance, following Masoud Barzani's warm welcome in Ankara in December 2015, the Islamic Republic News Agency angered Kurds by referring to the KRG president dismissively as the "northern Iraqi man in Kurdish trousers."[110] Kurds in both Iraq and Iran responded on social media by posting pictures of themselves proudly wearing Kurdish trousers.

Furthermore, Kurdish officials are concerned that Shi'a militias have become too powerful for Baghdad to control.[111] In March 2015, KRG Intelligence Chief Masrour Barzani warned that the Iraqi government's heavy reliance on Shi'a militias "could result in a problem even bigger than ISIL."[112] Shi'a militias have set up checkpoints between the Kurdish region and Baghdad, and have kidnapped several Kurdish truck drivers for ransom.[113] In October 2014, Asaib Ahl al-Haq militants loyal to Iran's Supreme Leader took the cousin of the Kurdish deputy prime minister hostage, demanding $1.7 million in ransom.[114] In Tuz Khurmato, which Iran-backed militias liberated from ISIL, peshmerga have confronted Shi'a militias over their treatment of Sunni Turkmen and Arabs, with one Kurdish officer referring to them as "the Shia Islamic State."[115] The town is one of several in Iraq that is under dispute regarding whether it should be part of Kurdish or Iraqi territory. In November 2015, Kurdish and Shi'a forces clashed for several days in Tuz Khurmato, leaving at least two Kurdish fight-

---

[109] The KRG also trucked 50,000 bpd to Turkey during the same period ("Kurdish History and Language According to Iran Draws KRG Protest," 2014).

[110] "Iran Worried by Kurdish Progress in the Region: KDPI," 2015.

[111] Vatanka and Shamsulddin, 2015.

[112] "Maghaam-e Kurdistan-e Aragh Dar Mowred-e Hamkari-ye Shebe Nezamiaan-e Shi'a ba Artesh Hoshdaar Daad [KRG Official Warns of Shi'a Militant Cooperation with Military]," 2015.

[113] Vatanka and Shamsulddin, 2015.

[114] "Baghdad Shootout Points to Growing Militia Threat," 2014.

[115] Quoted in Knodell, 2014.

ers, ten Shi'a militants, and six civilians dead.[116] Disagreement regarding control over oil-rich Kirkuk likely will be another major source of tension between the Kurds and Iraqi Shi'a in the event that ISIL is subdued. In June 2014, Asaib Ahl al-Haq head Qais al-Khazali warned that "Kirkuk is for all Iraqis. The insecurity in Iraq will end, and the Kurds shouldn't be taking advantage of the situation that has taken place."[117] In February 2015, at least 5,000 members of the Shi'a Popular Mobilization Forces set up a base six miles outside of the ethnically mixed city of Kirkuk, causing concern among the Kurds.[118] Masoud Barzani has said that Shi'a militia entry would be "prohibited under any circumstances."[119]

In the event that the KRG declares independence and fighting breaks out over Kirkuk, it is unclear whether Iran would see a benefit in supporting the Iraqis over the Kurds; from a purely strategic standpoint, if an independent Kurdish state was already established, which side controlled Kirkuk should not matter for Iran's economy or security.

Geopolitical Considerations

Iran's competition with its geopolitical rivals would largely influence its reaction to Kurdish independence. While the situation would not be ideal, Iran would not want to alienate the Erbil government and provide greater space for Turkey, the United States, and Israel to maneuver in a new country on its borders.

Turkish-Iranian relations have affected the Kurdish situation in much the same manner that Tehran's rivalry with the Ba'athist government of Saddam Hussein once did, with each country using the

[116] Qader, 2015; "Up to 18 Killed in Tuz Khurmatu Violence," 2015.

[117] Quoted in "Hoshdaar-e Dabir Kol-e Asa'ib Ahl al-Haq Darbaare-ye Su' Estefaade-ye Kurdha-ye Aragh [Head of Asa'ib Ahl al-Haq's Warning About Iraq's Kurds Taking Advantage]," 2014.

[118] Salama and Janssen, 2015.

[119] Quoted in Salama and Janssen, 2015.

various Kurdish parties to gain leverage over the other. In fact, it is a common assessment among Iranian officials that a major factor in Turkey's decisionmaking regarding potential Kurdish independence is Ankara's desire to counter Tehran.[120] According to Alex Vatanka, "The Iranians believe the Turks would rather see Iraq's Kurds break away than remain in a federal Iraq beholden to the Shi'a-led, Tehran-backed central government in Baghdad."[121] During the 1990s—despite a tacit agreement not to use Kurds directly as proxies against each other— Ankara and Tehran still supported each other's Kurdish enemies. The Turkish military, for instance, was known to leave arms unsecured in the vicinity of KDPI bases, while Iran allowed the PKK to operate in its territory.[122] The rise of the Islamist AKP in Ankara led to a thawing of tensions between Iran and Turkey, which affected the Kurds as well. Following Prime Minister Erdoğan's visit to Tehran in 2004, Iran declared the PKK a terrorist organization and promised to crack down on its activities.[123] However, increasing Turkish-Iranian rivalry in the past decade, much of it the result of the Syrian civil war, has made the AKP more reluctant to cooperate with Tehran in any shape or form in recent years.

Although they ceased support for opposition groups, Iran and Turkey began to compete for influence over the KRG as Ankara attempted to bring the Kurdish region under its orbit in order to counter Tehran's influence over Baghdad.[124] The economic sphere has been a major area of competition, with Turkey currently in the lead. As noted earlier, around 1,200 Turkish companies operate in Iraqi Kurdistan, dominating the construction and oil sector.[125] Meanwhile, the $12 billion in Turkish exports to the KRG is double Iran's overall trade with

---

[120] Vatanka, 2014.

[121] Vatanka, 2014.

[122] Yildiz and Taysi, 2007.

[123] Yildiz and Taysi, 2007.

[124] Tanchum, 2015a.

[125] Richards, 2013.

the Kurdistan Region.[126] Turkey's activities in Iraqi Kurdistan are part of its broader effort to diversify its source of energy resources, specifically to lessen its reliance on Iranian and Russian oil and gas.[127] The Iranian hardline conservative Mashregh News claims that Ankara has been meddling in Iraqi affairs and dealing with the KRG out of fear that a Kurdistan-Iraq-Syria pipeline would displace Turkey's importance as the hub for Mediterranean gas deliveries.[128] Iran also faces stiff competition with Turkey over cultural influence. In a July 2014 interview with Mashregh News, expert on Turkish affairs Mohammad Ali Dastmali castigated Iran for its "diplomatic and economic laziness," which has allowed the Turks to gain the advantage in the Kurdish cultural sphere.[129] Whereas a few years ago, a visitor to the Iraqi Kurdish region would hear Iranian music playing in people's cars, now Turkish music dominates. Dastmali also is concerned that many Kurdish youths are opting to learn Turkish rather than Persian. However, according to Ardeshir Pashang, visiting researcher at the Center for Middle East Strategic Studies in Tehran, effective cultural diplomacy could turn Iraqi Kurdish independence into an opportunity rather than a threat.[130] He suggests that Iran highlight its linguistic and cultural affinity with Kurds, including their shared tradition of Norouz, the Persian New Year. This would be similar to Turkey's strategy of promoting a Greater Turkistan that stretches from Anatolia to Mongolia.[131]

Despite their rivalry, the Iranian consensus appears to be that Turkey will not go so far as to support Kurdish independence. According to a Mashregh analysis, Turkey's interest in maintaining economic relations with Iran is high enough that it would not jeopardize it in

---

[126] Tanchum, 2015a.

[127] Jenkins, 2013.

[128] "Tahlil-e Raftari-ye Kurdha-ye Aragh [Behavioral Analysis of Iraq's Kurds]," 2014.

[129] "Esteghlaal-e Aghliim-e Kurdistan-e Aragh Dar Kootah Modat Namomken Ast [Independence of Iraq's Kurdish Region Not Possible in Short Term]," 2014.

[130] Pashang, 2014.

[131] Pashang, 2014.

favor of the Kurds.[132] Furthermore, some Iranian analysts argue, the Turks would not want to upset NATO members, who do not support Kurdish independence. Therefore, the most Turkey would do is not object to independence.

Iranians are divided over Washington's end goals regarding the Kurds. Some believe U.S. statements that Washington does not support the creation of an independent Kurdistan. Kayhan Barzegar, head of the Center for Scientific Research and Middle East Strategic Studies in Tehran, has argued that this poses a great impediment to the Kurds declaring independence.[133] Others, however, see nefarious U.S. motives. For instance, the conservative newspaper *Jomhouri Eslami* characterized Masoud Barzani's June 2014 call for a referendum as part of a U.S. conspiracy to break Iraq up into "bite-sized" pieces that could be more easily dominated.[134]

There is a consensus over Israel's goals, however. Foreign Ministry Spokeswoman Marzieh Afkham referred to Barzani's referendum call as "a Zionist conspiracy."[135] Hardline Ayatollah Ahmad Khatami warned that a Kurdish state would "become another cancerous tumor like Israel."[136] And a Fars News analysis claimed that the creation of Kurdistan was part of Israel's long-term plan to create a "Greater Israel," and that Kurdistan would provide a base for Israeli espionage.[137]

Iranian Reactions to Kurdish Independence

The consensus among analysts in Iran appears to be that Iraq's Kurds will not declare independence in the short term, although they con-

---

[132] "Ellat-e Hemayat-e Ankara Az Esteghlaal-e Aghlim-e Kurdistan Chiist? [What Are Reasons Behind Turkey's Support for Kurdistan's Independence?]," 2014.

[133] Barzegar, 2014a.

[134] "Safar-e Vazir Khareje-ye Amrika va Tote'e-ye Tajzie-ye Aragh [U.S. Secretary of State's Visit and Conspiracy to Split Up Iraq]," 2014.

[135] Quoted in Namazi, 2014.

[136] Quoted in Namazi, 2014.

[137] Zaraei, 2015.

sider that Masoud Barzani's ultimate goal is independence. There are divisions, however, on the impact that Kurdish independence would have on Iran.

Most analysts interviewed by the Iranian press assess that Barzani's announcement of a referendum on independence was intended to gain concessions from Baghdad—gains that could set the stage for independence down the road.[138] Along the same lines, according to the Iranians, the Kurds also have used the excuse of defending against ISIL to take over disputed land, such as Kirkuk.[139] Barzegar argues that Western and regional pressure to not declare independence will have a dampening effect on Kurdish efforts—especially in light of the fact that the KRG military is so reliant on the United States and Iran for help against ISIL.[140] The KRG may worry about the effect that lack of international support would have on would-be investors and the enthusiasm of tourists to visit an independent Kurdistan. Barzegar also assesses that Barzani's call for a referendum may have backfired and put independence back at least a decade; the lack of international support for his statement was apparent, and the ensuing arguments between Kurdish factions highlighted the fact that Erbil and Sulaimaniyah were not on the same page regarding the pace and process for achieving independence.[141]

While Iranian officials are undoubtedly concerned about the ramifications that Kurdish independence would have on Iran, there is little public discussion about the specificity of the threats it would pose—most likely due to the sensitive nature of the topic. Some news articles have expressed concern over general "security threats" that could

---

[138] "Esteghlaal-e Aghliim-e Kurdistan-e Aragh Dar Kootah Modat Namomken Ast [Independence of Iraq's Kurdish Region Not Possible in Short Term]," 2014; "Aragh va Sooda-ye Esteghlaal-Talabi-ye Aghliim-e Kurdistan [Iraq and Kurdistan Region's Independence Aspirations]," 2014.

[139] "Aragh va Sooda-ye Esteghlaal-Talabi-ye Aghliim-e Kurdistan [Iraq and Kurdistan Region's Independence Aspirations]," 2014.

[140] Barzegar, 2014a.

[141] Barzegar, 2014b.

result from Iraqi Kurdish independence.[142] However, there is a lack of analysis in Iranian newspapers or publicly available think tank publications that discuss the impact that KRG independence would have on Iran's Kurds. In a 2008 op-ed, Mohammad Ali Sobhani, Iran's former ambassador to Lebanon, expressed concerns likely shared by security officials that a partitioned Iraq could weaken the Islamic Republic's regional position.[143] With three small countries resulting from fragmentation, outside powers would find it easier to manipulate each one. Moreover, argued Sobhani, a united Iraq is to Iran's benefit because Iraq's Shi'a need Tehran to help them balance against Sunni Arabs and the Kurds. In the event of fragmentation, an independent Shi'a Iraq would not need Iran's help in domestic politics, and Arab nationalist feelings could take over.[144]

Several reformist-leaning analysts have pushed back against the notion that Kurdish independence would pose a threat. They note that the KRG has clamped down on the Iranian Kurdish opposition operating on its soil.[145] On the other hand, when Baghdad has had control over northern Iraq, it has used the Kurds against Iran.[146] It has also been argued that Iran would not fare the worst out of all the regional powers. According to Abdollah Ramazanzadeh, a Kurdish academic, and former member of the Khatami administration, the Shi'a and Kurdish countries bordering Iran would be oil-rich, while the Sunni country bordering Turkey would be relatively poor (and thus be more prone to instability).[147] Reformist-leaning analyst Pashang argues that, with forward-thinking policies, Iran could even turn Iraqi Kurdish

---

[142] Vatanka, 2014.

[143] "Sobhani, Mohammad Ali. "Kodam Aragh Manafe-ye Iran ra Ta'miin Mikonad? [Which Iraq Will Secure Iran's Interests?]," 2008.

[144] "Sobhani, Mohammad Ali. "Kodam Aragh Manafe-ye Iran ra Ta'miin Mikonad? [Which Iraq Will Secure Iran's Interests?]," 2008.

[145] Pashang, 2014.

[146] "Tajzie-ye Aragh: Sood Ya Zian-e Iran? [Partition of Iraq: Iran's Benefit or Loss?]," 2014.

[147] "Tajzie-ye Aragh: Sood Ya Zian-e Iran? [Partition of Iraq: Iran's Benefit or Loss?]," 2014.

independence into an opportunity rather than a threat.[148] He believes that Iran cannot rely solely on close relations with the Shi'a Baghdad government. Due to geopolitical reasons, writes Pashang, Iraq "has always been, and always will be, a rival of Iran's"—regardless of who is in power.[149] He also has made the rare recommendation that Iran invest in the economy of its Kurdish region and appoint Kurds to senior government positions in order to counter the possible allure of an independent Kurdistan.[150]

Iran's hard-liners, however, are likely to view the Kurds as a security threat regardless.[151] Mashregh News, for instance, warned in August 2014 that the Kurds should realize that Kurdistan and Iran share a long border, and Tehran has means "all along this border to exert pressure on a very small and weak neighbor."[152]

Unilateral Declaration of Kurdish Independence

The abrupt nature of a unilateral declaration as well as a standoff between Baghdad and the Kurds would likely empower Iranians who see Iran's Kurdish situation solely through a security lens, sidelining pragmatists who would prefer to address the challenge by improving the lives of Iranian minorities.

Tehran's threat perception would be exacerbated by a strong Iranian Kurdish reaction to Erbil's announcement. In the face of international opposition to Kurdish independence, Iran's Kurds likely might engage in public support for Erbil in a more intense manner than would otherwise be the case. In this regard, the stark difference in the level of Iranian Kurdish public support for Kurds under threat in Kobane versus those who won in Turkey's parliamentary election is illustrative. In the event of large demonstrations, the inevitable harsh secu-

---

[148] Pashang, 2014.

[149] Pashang, 2014.

[150] Pashang, 2014.

[151] Bozorgmehr, 2014a.

[152] "Ellat-e Hemayat-e Ankara Az Esteghlaal-e Aghlim-e Kurdistan Chiist? [What Are Reasons Behind Turkey's Support for Kurdistan's Independence?]," 2014.

rity crackdown on these demonstrators would further reinforce Iranian Kurdish nationalist sentiment.

Skirmishes between the Iraqi government and the Kurds likely would intensify the level of protests inside Iran. Furthermore, an Erbil preoccupied with fighting Baghdad's forces could provide the space for Iranian Kurdish militants based in the Qandil Mountains to operate more freely. And if Iran's Kurdish region were to become destabilized in the face of mass protests and crackdowns, KDPI and Komala could reactivate their militant activities. For its part, Iran may resume its attempts to assassinate Iranian Kurdish dissidents in Iraq.

While Iran most likely would attempt to convince its PUK allies to push for reconciliation with Baghdad, Erbil's disputes with the Iraqi government over territory coupled with the international community's reluctance to accept a Kurdish state could unite the KDP and PUK, thus limiting Tehran's influence over the Kurds.

The level of Iran's economic engagement with an independent Kurdistan would be influenced in large part by Turkey's activities there. If Turkey slowed its rate of investment in the Kurdish region in the face of Iraqi pressure, Iran could similarly refrain from increasing its business presence there. However, if Turkey were to ignore Iraq's protests, Iran could view ceding economic territory to its Turkish rival as more harmful than angering an Iraqi government over which it nonetheless already has a great deal of influence. In that case, Iran likely would still seek to extract concessions from Erbil—for instance, demanding high transit fees to transport Kurdish oil through Iranian territory.

Tehran may be tempted to react physically to a unilateral declaration of independence by the KRG; while Iran is unlikely to send troops into the KRG, it could nevertheless mobilize surrogates to conduct attacks against KRG targets. This scenario, however, is not a given; even Tehran's vehement opposition to a unilateral KRG declaration of independence would be tempered by close economic, political, and security ties to a number of Kurdish actors, especially the PUK. Moreover, Tehran would like to maintain good relations with the KRG as a way to balance against Iran's regional competitors, especially Turkey.

Gradual Estrangement

In light of the relatively managed and predictable nature of Kurdish independence in this scenario, Iranian strategists would have had time to plan. Therefore, Iran's threat perception could be lower than in other situations. As a result, pragmatists likely would be empowered to advocate for cordial relations with a new Kurdish state and to push for domestic economic development and political reforms aimed at lessening Iranian Kurdish attraction to the new state.

Among Iran's Kurds, those living in the areas of Sanandaj and Kermanshah would be the most likely to hold public celebrations following Iraqi Kurdish independence. Demonstrations could be smaller in Orumieh and other parts of northern Iranian Kurdistan, where the residents do not have close ties with Kurds in Iraq. However, if Iranian forces cracked down on the celebrations, it likely would ignite demonstrations throughout Iranian Kurdistan. A measured Iranian reaction to Kurdish independence would lessen the chance that Kurdish militant violence would increase. Furthermore, a stable Erbil government would continue to limit anti-Iranian Kurdish activities on its soil.

Iran would focus on maintaining its leverage with the PUK as a means of countering the KDP's close ties with Turkey. However, Tehran would be careful to not become estranged from the Erbil government, lest it open the space for Kurdistan-based U.S. and Israeli activities against Iran. Moreover, Iran would want cordial ties with Erbil in order to compete economically with Turkey, especially in the fields of construction and energy. This would likely remain the case even in the event that the Kurds came into conflict with Baghdad over control of Kirkuk. Finally, in the event that a strengthened Iraq becomes more independent from Iran, Tehran would likely see the benefit of having a strong Kurdistan to balance against it.

Last Man Standing

In this scenario, with a failing Iraq state next door, and with Iran likely increasingly engaged in holding Iraq together, hardline factions would hold sway over Tehran's policy toward the Kurds. Therefore, Iran's response to Kurdish independence would be viewed solely through a security prism, with likely little attention paid to economic development opportunities or local grievances.

A continued ISIL threat against Iraq's Kurds would increase the likelihood of large Iranian Kurdish demonstrations in support of the new Kurdish state. These demonstrations most likely would be met with force, ultimately reinforcing Kurdish nationalist sentiment. If unrest were to spread in Iran's Kurdish region, the KDPI and Komala could decide to resume their militant activities. An Erbil government distracted by conflicts with ISIL and Baghdad could leave more room for Iranian groups to operate from its soil. For its part, Iran could respond by targeting Iranian dissidents based in Sulaimaniyah. Meanwhile, ISIL's continued success likely would empower Kurdish Sunni Islamists, who could begin conducting attacks against Iranian government targets.

While Iran would prefer a Kurdish government that is stable enough to help counter ISIL and rein in Iranian dissidents on its soil, it would not want it strong enough to counter its Iraqi satellite state. Tehran likely would attempt to use its ties to the PUK to lessen tensions between Erbil and Baghdad; however, the instability likely will have brought the KDP and PUK closer together, decreasing Iran's ability to exert influence. The Iranians would still seek to increase their economic activities in a new Kurdish state, largely to counter Turkey's influence there. But potential clashes between Kurdish peshmerga and Shi'a militias would sour Tehran-Erbil relations, which could push the Kurds even closer to Ankara both politically and economically.

The Influence of Kurdish Nationalism

Pan-Kurdish nationalism emanating from an independent Kurdistan would lead Iranian hard-liners to monopolize control over Tehran's policy regarding the Kurds.

Iran's security forces would likely greet any public display of support for Erbil among Iranian Kurds with a swift and harsh response. This would occur despite the fact that most Kurds in Iran probably would not identify with Iraqi Kurdish officials as potential leaders of their community. Moreover, the Iranian Kurdish political parties would likely see Erbil's action as an attempt by Barzani's KDP to usurp their power. Ultimately, a harsh Iranian crackdown in its Kurdish region—coupled with the desire of the KDPI, Komala, and the PJAK to outshine the KDP—would increase the likelihood of large-scale militant activities inside Iran.

Erbil-inspired unrest in Iran could incentivize Tehran to destabilize the new Kurdish state. Space for meddling would open up for Iran if the PUK decided that Barzani was attempting to sideline it by claiming to lead all Kurds. Ultimately, Tehran would be likely to decrease its economic activities in the Kurdish region, despite the risk of ceding ground to Turkey in that arena. Iran may even consider closing its borders to the KRG and imposing an economic embargo if the KRG should espouse pan-Kurdish nationalism (though in such an event, Turkey would also take action, making this an unlikely eventuality). Tehran would also likely take Baghdad's reservations about an independent Kurdistan more seriously.

Conclusion

Iranian officials have made clear their opposition to an independent Kurdistan, but they are unlikely to actively oppose a new Kurdish state on Iran's borders in an overly forceful manner. A desire to counter Turkish, U.S., and Israeli influence over Erbil coupled with the economic opportunities provided by having a landlocked neighbor in need of an outlet for its exports will serve as factors mitigating potentially reflexive Iranian opposition. The reaction of Iranian Kurds to an independent Kurdistan in northern Iran may be a decisive factor in shaping Tehran's policies.

In relation to Kurdish independence, the best scenario for the KRG would be Erbil's announcement of independence at the end of drawn-out discussions with Baghdad. The lack of strategic surprise would increase the chance that Iranian pragmatists would have a say in Tehran's strategy, leading to an approach prizing diplomacy with the KRG in addition to economic development of Iran's Kurdish regions, as opposed to further militarization of Kurdish inhabited areas. The manner in which Erbil declares independence is important because of the impact it would have on Iran's threat perception, which is colored in large part by its preconceptions regarding its own Kurdish population. An abrupt, destabilizing partitioning of Iraq or a Barzani-led state claiming the mantle of pan-Kurdish nationalism would make any Iranian Kurdish celebration of Erbil's independence seem all the more threatening—despite the fact that the level of affinity toward a new Erbil government likely would vary by location within Iran as well as political ideology. Harsh crackdowns on the celebrations could intensify Kurdish nationalism at a time when Iran's Kurdish youths are focusing much of their political activities on broader civil society, rather than ethnic issues. In an increasingly securitized atmosphere, the currently weak foreign-based Iranian Kurdish political parties could regain their strength, perhaps even intensifying their militias' resistance against the state. Ultimately, in treating its Kurdish population as a persistent security threat, Iran could bring about the very conditions it seeks to prevent.

The successful implementation of the Joint Comprehensive Plan of Action nuclear deal between Iran and the P5+1 (United States, Russia, China, United Kingdom, France, and Germany) could have lasting implications for the entire Middle East. An Iran relieved of sanctions will be free to intensify its investments in a new Kurdish state, likely focusing on the energy industry as well as construction of a rail network to further integrate the two economies. In the event that the nuclear agreement falls apart, hard-liners in Iran likely will succeed in sidelining pragmatists in Tehran, decreasing the chance that Iranian Kurdish grievances will be addressed.

CHAPTER SIX

Conclusion

An independent Kurdistan would be a major event in an increasingly unstable Middle East. The birth of a new Kurdish nation would, if it occurred, face strong opposition from the Iraqi central government in Baghdad and perhaps some of Iraq's hard-line backers in Tehran. However, an independent Kurdistan in northern Iraq may be greeted warmly by Turkey, and may even come to be tolerated by Baghdad and Tehran under certain circumstances. The KRG's success in tamping down opposition to independence may be in large part shaped by scenarios under which Erbil declares independence: A sudden unilateral declaration is likely to provoke regional opposition, whereas a negotiated and/or gradual estrangement between Baghdad and Erbil may minimize opposition to an independent state.

Baghdad's response to the emergence of a Kurdish nation in northern Iraq would likely vary considerably depending on how Kurdistan is established. Ironically, many of the measures Baghdad could take to punish the Kurds for unilaterally declaring independence would be the natural outcome of the KRG gaining independence through the collapse of the Iraqi state. In both cases, the newly established Kurdistan would be forced to cope with financial difficulties, social upheaval as refugees flow across the Iraqi-Kurdish border, and isolation from any markets in Baghdad-controlled Iraq to which it previously had access. Such serious challenges would strain the new nation, which could influence the KRG's cost-benefit analysis of whether and how to fulfill its long sought-after goal of independence.

Kurdish independence achieved through a negotiated separation between Baghdad and Erbil ultimately offers the greatest potential benefits for both Iraq and Kurdistan. An amicable divorce, whether against the central government's wishes or not, would enable Baghdad to mitigate the negative consequences of Kurdish independence. For example, Baghdad could negotiate with the Kurds for access to pipelines leading to Turkey from oilfields along Iraq's new northern border, which could pave the way for future cooperation in oil exports. Furthermore, Baghdad could ease the transition of peshmerga serving in the Iraqi Army as they reintegrate into Kurdish forces. This could facilitate future security cooperation, which would be crucial to Iraqi and Kurdish efforts to repel ISIL and contain Syria's instability from spilling across the border. While Baghdad may be reluctant to enable Kurdish independence in this scenario, the Iraqi government could decide that the long-term benefits of a cooperative Kurdistan outweigh the short-term political costs of Kurdish secession.

Baghdad's potential response likely will factor into the KRG's determination of whether to pursue independence at any given time. As the ramifications of independence initiated through a unilateral declaration are potentially severe, the Kurds may be less likely to pursue sovereignty in that fashion. Baghdad and Erbil seem willing to negotiate yet more agreements on revenue-sharing, oil exports, disputed territories, and other unresolved issues, despite the fact that few of these arrangements have yet to hold. The two capitals could continue such efforts to maintain the status quo, or—tired from the perpetual uncertainty created by ongoing disagreements—they could eventually decide to pursue a negotiated separation that enables both to pursue their interests.

Turkey has made a series of strategic decisions that have led it to a point where support for an independent Kurdish state may be its logical outcome. Turkey's efforts to resolve its internal Kurdish insurgency—despite the resumption of violence in 2015—have virtually eliminated the chance that Turkish Kurds would secede and removed the irredentist threat posed by the emergence of an independent Kurdish state to Turkey's southeast. Ankara's decisions to resume armed conflict with the PKK are unlikely to alter Turkey's strong political, economic, and commercial interests in close ties with the KRG, which would likely grow closer—and advance Turkey's interests even further—if the KRG were to secure independence. Economic opportunity, and political frustrations and security concerns regarding the Shi'a-dominated Baghdad government, have led Turkey to develop close political and economic ties with the KRG, transforming Ankara from Erbil's most vociferous critic into Erbil's greatest partner. Turkey's political outreach to the KRG leadership has helped constrain the PKK's military capabilities and provided indirect influence over Syrian Kurdish groups whose territorial control could serve as a base for a renewed insurgency against Turkey. Rapidly growing bilateral trade and investment have contributed to economic growth in both Turkey and the KRG, and mutual energy-related interests—Erbil needs to sell to someone other than Baghdad, and Turkey is eager to meet its growing domestic energy needs—have reinforced close economic, commercial, and political ties.

Turkey is not explicitly eager to see the KRG declare independence, particularly if the KRG's secession from Iraq could generate even greater instability in central and southern Iraq. That said, Kurdish independence would likely be advantageous to Turkey. An independent Kurdistan recognized by the international community would be far freer to develop its energy resources without legal hurdles or interference from Baghdad, and Turkey would be a leading player in an independent Kurdistan's hydrocarbons sector. Turkey would also be much freer to provide security assistance to a sovereign Kurdish state, which shares Ankara's interests in pushing ISIL out of Kurdish territory, without alienating Baghdad. This combination of expanding political, economic, and security ties between Ankara and Erbil would make Turkey an independent Kurdistan's closest and most important ally.

Turkey would prefer that the KRG pursue a gradual path toward independence so as not to further destabilize the Iraqi central government, halt oil production while sovereignty and ownership of hydrocarbon resources are resolved, or introduce a potentially controversial issue into Turkish domestic politics. But even an abrupt declaration of independence by Iraqi Kurdish leaders—whether unilaterally or in response to a rapidly declining security situation in Iraq—likely would be endorsed by Turkey, as the strategic gains of diplomatic recognition would outweigh the near-term cost of Baghdad's distress. Turkey will likely be one of the first countries to recognize an independent Kurdistan no matter how Kurdish sovereignty is achieved.

Iran would oppose Kurdish independence on principle, but in reality it may tolerate an independent Kurdistan in northern Iraq if Iran judges it would not threaten its own stability. In particular, Tehran would be concerned about the reaction of Iranian Kurds to the KRG becoming an independent state. Iran's Kurdish population is not monolithic, and many Iranian Kurds may choose not to support an independent Kurdistan for cultural or political reasons. But Iran's Kurdish population is deeply disenfranchised; elements of Iran's Kurdish population may be inspired by an independent Kurdistan next door, and may even take up arms against the central government in Tehran. But a KRG that does not promote pan-Kurdish nationalism and is instead careful of Iranian interests may find some sympathy in Tehran, particularly among more pragmatic figures who see an independent Kurdistan as an opportunity for Iran.

After all, Iran maintains close economic, political, and security ties to the KRG and has long-standing ties to both the PUK and the KDP. In the past few years, Iran has increased its economic activities in the KRG and has helped the peshmerga push back ISIL forces from Kurdish territory. Iran is wary of Turkish, Israeli, and U.S. influence in the KRG and wants to make sure that the KRG is not used as a future base for attacks or espionage against Iran. Therefore, Iran can tolerate an independent Kurdistan if it does not espouse pan-Kurdish ideology that could threaten Iran's stability while maintaining close security and economic ties with Tehran. From the Iranian government's perspective, a gradual and preferably negotiated Kurdish separation from Iraq would be preferable, as it would decrease Baghdad's objections to Kurdish independence and provide Tehran with the time necessary to mitigate potential unrest at home.

Kurdish independence would have a range of implications for U.S. interests if it were to occur. Iraqi Kurdistan has been a close U.S. partner since the first Gulf War in 1991, and the United States would certainly welcome greater political stability and economic growth in the Kurdistan Region. To the extent that independence would enable Erbil to enhance its defense and security posture, principally through the establishment of bilateral defense relationships with the United States, Turkey, and EU nations, the Kurdistan Region could help halt the advance of ISIL and the spread of instability from Syria and central Iraq. Finally, expanded trade and investment between an independent Kurdistan and Turkey, which would be the new country's most important economic partner, would help draw the new state into the orbit of a NATO ally.

On the other hand, Kurdish secession from Iraq could destabilize the rump Iraqi state politically, economically, and militarily—a result that is certainly not in the interests of the United States, which spent billions of dollars and thousands of lives in an effort to bring democracy and security to Iraq. Once the Kurds no longer participate in Iraqi politics as somewhat of a third-party balancing force, Sunni and Shi'a politicians will be thrown into a more direct competition for influence and spoils. The vacuum left by the Kurds, and the stakes of the resulting Sunni-Shi'a competition, could provide an opening for Tehran to expand its influence in Baghdad. Economically, Kurdish secession could cut Baghdad off from trade with Turkey, including, most importantly, the ability to export oil north through Turkey and onward to Europe through the Mediterranean. Baghdad would also lose financially, as it earned more money from the KRG's oil export revenues than it paid out to the KRG through the revenue-sharing agreement (particularly since Baghdad rarely paid its obligation in full). The effectiveness of the Iraqi military could decline as well; despite the many challenges associated with the coordination of Kurdish peshmerga with the Iraqi Security Forces, the peshmerga were often more effective fighters than the ISF in the fight against ISIL. If an independent Kurdish state's security forces protect only Kurdish territory from ISIL and other forces of instability, attackers may focus their offensives on the weaker ISF and move toward Baghdad rather than Erbil. Such developments could significantly weaken what remains of the Iraqi state, which could create yet another power vacuum, sectarian conflict, or opportunity for Iran to expand its influence in the region.

Nearly a century after the Sykes-Picot Agreement divided the Kurds of the Ottoman Empire among British and French protectorates, the Kurds of northern Iraq continue to pursue an independent state. Such a new country has no guarantees of success, however, unless the support of neighboring countries enables it to build strong political institutions, grow its economy, and guarantee its security. Turkey and Iran—which may conclude that an independent Kurdistan does not pose a threat to their own territorial integrity—may accept Kurdish independence under certain circumstances. Iraq is likely to be hostile to a unilateral declaration of Kurdish independence but may be too internally divided to stop it and may find benefits from negotiating a peaceful secession that advances Baghdad's and Erbil's mutual interests.

But while the Kurds have focused on the establishment of a sovereign state as their principal goal, a declaration of independence would only be the initial step in the building of a new nation. As many other nations have learned, constructing a stable, prosperous state is far more complicated than proclaiming its existence.

Abbreviations

AKP	Justice and Development Party
bpd	barrels per day
CPA	Coalition Provisional Authority
DTP	Democratic Society Party
HDP	People's Democratic Party
IDP	internally displaced person
IOC	international oil company
IRGC	Islamic Revolutionary Guards Corps
ISF	Iraqi Security Forces
ISIL	Islamic State of Iraq and Levant
ISIS	Islamic State of Iraq and Syria
KDP	Kurdistan Democratic Party
KDPI	Kurdish Democratic Party of Iran
KGK	Kurdistan People's Congress
KRG	Kurdistan Regional Government
OFFP	Oil for Food Program
PJAK	Party of Free Life of Kurdistan

PKK	Kurdistan Workers' Party
PUK	Patriotic Union of Kurdistan
PYD	Democratic Union Party
SOMO	State Organization for Marketing of Oil
TAL	Transitional Administrative Law
UN	United Nations
YPG	Syrian Kurdish People's Protection Units

References

"After Training Peshmerga, Turkey Now Set to Train and Equip FSA with US," *Daily Sabah*, November 26, 2014.

Ahmadzadeh, Hashem, and Gareth Stansfield, "The Political, Cultural, and Military Re-Awakening of the Kurdish Nationalist Movement in Iran," *Middle East Journal*, Vol. 64, No. 1, 2010, pp. 11–27.

Ahmed, Hevidar, "Iran Calls the Shots on PUK Leadership Issue," *Rudaw*, May 23, 2013.

Ahmed, Hunar, "Official: Peshmerga Control 90 Percent of 140 Previously 'Arabicized' Zones," *Rudaw*, April 28, 2015. As of May 4, 2016: http://rudaw.net/english/kurdistan/280420151

Ahmed, Mohammed M. A., *Iraqi Kurds and Nation-Building*, New York: Palgrave Macmillan, 2012.

Aktan, Irfan, "What's behind AKP's Allegations of Gulen-PKK Ties?" *Al-Monitor*, August 15, 2016. As of September 15, 2016: http://www.al-monitor.com/pulse/originals/2016/08/ turkey-why-erdogan-wants-link-gulen-pkk.html

Akyol, Mustafa, "How the AKP Dominated Yesterday's Election in Turkey," *Al-Monitor*, November 2, 2015. As of September 19, 2016: http://www.al-monitor.com/pulse/originals/2015/11/ turkey-elections-akp-unexpected-victory-erdogan.html

"Al-Maliki Rules Out Poll on Kurdish Independence," *Hurriyet Daily News*, 2014.

Allam, Hannah, Jonathan S. Landay, and Warren P. Strobel, "Iranian Outmaneuvers U.S. in Iraq," *McClatchy News*, April 28, 2008.

Allawi, Ali A., *The Occupation of Iraq: Winning the War, Losing the Peace*, New Haven, Conn.: Yale University Press, 2008.

Aqrawi, Shamal "Investment a 'Success Story' in Iraqi Kurdistan," Reuters, September 29, 2010.

"Aragh va Sooda-ye Esteghlaal-Talabi-ye Aghliim-e Kurdistan [Iraq and Kurdistan Region's Independence Aspirations]," *Islamic Republic News Agency*, July 12, 2014.

Arango, Tim, and Clifford Krauss, "Kurds' Oil Deals with Turkey Raise Fears of Fissures in Iraq," *New York Times*, December 2, 2013.

Arslan, Deniz, "Turkey Against Enforcing Solution in Kirkuk Unilaterally," *Today's Zaman*, June 30, 2014.

Aslan, Ali H., "PM Erdoğan, EU Bid Behind Turkey's Civilianization," *Today's Zaman*, August 4, 2011.

"Baghdad Shootout Points to Growing Militia Threat," *Al-Monitor*, October 21, 2014.

Baker, James A., Lee H. Hamilton, Lawrence S. Eagleburger, Vernon E. Jordan, Edwin Meese, Sandra Day O'Connor, Leon E. Panetta, William J. Perry, Charles S. Robb, and Alan K. Simpson, *The Iraq Study Group Report*, Washington, D.C.: U.S. Institute of Peace, 2006.

Barkey, Henri J., *Turkey's New Engagement in Iraq*, Washington, D.C.: U.S. Institute of Peace, 2010.

———, "Kurds Are Now Key to a Middle East Solution," Wilson Center, February 26, 2016.

Barkey, Henri J., and Graham E. Fuller, *Turkey's Kurdish Question*, Lanham, Md.: Rowman & Littlefield Publishers, 1998.

"Barzani and Erdoğan Open Erbil Int'l Airport and Turkish Consulate," *Iraq Business News*, March 31, 2011.

"Barzani: Iran Gave Weapons to Iraq's Kurds," *Al Arabiya News*, August 26, 2014.

Barzegar, Kayhan, *Da'esh Yek Ejmaa-e Siyaasi va E'telaaf-e Kootah Modat [Da'esh a Short-Term Political Consensus and Coalition]*, Tehran: Center for Scientific Research and Middle East Strategic Research, 2014a.

———, *Tahavolaat-e Akhiir-e Aragh va Amniyat-e Melli-ye Iran [Iraq's Latest Transformations and Iran's National Security]*, Tehran: Center for Scientific Research and Middle East Strategic Studies, 2014b.

Baydar, Yavus, "Kurdish Independence Seems Inevitable, but Problematic," *Today's Zaman*, July 8, 2014.

Beehner, Lionel, *The Iraqi Kurdish Question*, Washington, D.C.: Council on Foreign Relations, 2007.

Bekdil, Burak Ege, "Turkey, US Agree to Train and Arm Syrian Opposition," *Defense News*, November 24, 2014.

Bonfield, Craig, *Kurdish Push for Independence Derailed by ISIL?* Washington, D.C.: Center for Strategic and International Studies, 2014.

Bozarslan, Hamit, "Kurds: States, Marginality, and Security," in Sam C. Nolutshungu, ed., *Margins of Insecurity: Minorities and International Security*, Rochester, N.Y.: University of Rochester Press, 1996.

———, "Kurds and the Turkish State," in Resat Kasaba, ed., *The Cambridge History of Turkey*, Cambridge, UK.: Cambridge University Press, 2008.

Bozorgmehr, Najmeh, "Iran's Kurds Seek Coexistence with Shia as Life Improves," *Financial Times*, December 3, 2014a.

———, "Border Town in Iranian Kurdistan Booms Through Trade with Iraq," *Financial Times*, December 18, 2014b.

"Brawl Erupts over Word 'Kurdistan' in Turkish Parliament," *Today's Zaman*, 2013.

Brennan, Richard, Charles P. Ries, Larry Hanauer, Ben Connable, Terrence K. Kelly, Michael J. McNerney, Stephanie Young, Jason H. Campbell, and K. Scott McMahon, *Ending the U.S. War in Iraq: The Final Transition, Operational Maneuver, and Disestablishment of United States Forces–Iraq*, Santa Monica, Calif.: RAND Corporation, RR-232-SFI, 2013. As of May 4, 2016: http://www.rand.org/pubs/research_reports/RR232.html

Bruinessen, Martin Van, "Major Kurdish Organizations in Iran," *Middle East Report*, Vol. 16, July/August 1986.

Çağaptay, Soner, "Turkey's Kurdish Buffer," *Foreign Affairs*, July 1, 2014.

———, "Implications of Turkey's War Against the PKK," Washington Institute for Near Eastern Affairs, Policy Watch #2470, August 14, 2015. As of April 25, 2016: http://www.washingtoninstitute.org/policy-analysis/view/ implications-of-turkeys-war-against-the-pkk

Çağaptay, Soner, Christina Bache Fidan, and Ege Cansu Sacikara, *Turkey and the KRG: An Undeclared Economic Commonwealth*, Washington, D.C.: Washington Institute for Near East Policy, 2015.

Çağaptay, Soner, Caitlin Stull, and Mark Bhaskar, "Turkey's Political Uncertainty: Implications of the June 2015 Parliamentary Elections," Washington Institute for Near East Policy Research Notes, No. 27, August 2015, p. 1. As of April 25, 2016: http://www.washingtoninstitute.org/policy-analysis/view/ turkeys-political-uncertainty

Caglayan, Selin, "Turkish Investments and Trade Undeterred by Erbil Attack," *Rudaw*, October 4, 2013.

Çamlıbel, Cansu, "Analyst: Both PKK and AKP Want HDP to Be Weakened," *Hurriyet Daily News*, September 16, 2015. As of April 25, 2016: http://www.hurriyetdailynews.com/analyst-both-pkk-and-akp-want-hdp-to-be-weakened-.aspx?PageID=238&NID=88554&NewsCatID=338

Chomani, Kamal, "Push for Kurdish Independence Divides Iraqi Kurds," *Al-Monitor*, July 9, 2014.

Cole, Juan, "Kurdish General Again Insubordinate, Angles for US to Remain in Iraq," *Informed Comment*, August 13, 2010. As of May 4, 2016: http://www.juancole.com/2010/08/kurdish-general-again-insubordinate-angles-for-us-to-remain-in-iraq.html

Colombo, Jesse, "Why the Worst Is Still Ahead for Turkey's Bubble Economy," *Forbes*, March 5, 2014.

"Crowded by Two Shaky States, Turkey Shifts Its Weight in Policy," *All Things Considered*, National Public Radio, June 26, 2014.

Dagher, Sam, "Iraq's Simmering Ethnic War over Kirkuk," *Christian Science Monitor*, April 24, 2008.

Dastmali, Mohammad Ali, "Fasli Noiin Dar Ravabet-e Iran va Aghliim-e Kurdistan-e Aragh [New Season in Relations Between Iran and Iraqi Kurdistan]," *IR Diplomacy*, January 1, 2015.

"Davutoğlu Says Turkey Not Against Kurdish Autonomy in Post-Assad Syria," *Today's Zaman*, August 9, 2012.

Democratic Party of Iranian Kurdistan, "High-Level Meeting Between KDPI and Komala," undated.

———, "Yearly Human Rights Report: 956 Kurds Imprisoned and 206 Were Killed or Injured by Iran," March 27, 2015a. As of April 25, 2016: http://pdki.org/english/yearly-human-rights-report-956-kurds-imprisoned-and-206-were-killed-or-injured-by-iran

———, "Three Revolutionary Guards Killed and Two Injured in Armed Clashes in Eastern Kurdistan," May 29, 2015b. As of April 25, 2016: http://pdki.org/english/three-revolutionary-guards-killed-and-two-injured-in-armed-clashes-in-eastern-kurdistan

———, "Ahmedi: PDKI's Peshmerga Forces Will Defend the Kurdish People Against Iranian Aggression," May 31, 2015c. As of April 25, 2016: http://pdki.org/english/ahmedi-pdkis-peshmerga-forces-will-defend-the-kurdish-people-against-iranian-aggression

———, "Presence of PDKI's Peshmerga Forces Makes Iranian Regime Nervous," June 8, 2015d. As of April 25, 2016: http://pdki.org/english/presence-of-pdkis-peshmerga-forces-makes-iranian-regime-nervous

———, "Six Iranian Islamic Revolutionary Guards Killed in Kurdistan," June 10, 2015e. As of April 25, 2016: http://pdki.org/english/six-iranian-islamic-revolutionary-guards-killed-in-kurdistan

———, "Iran Increases Its Military Presence, Security Official Shot in Saqez," June 14, 2015f. As of April 25, 2016:
http://pdki.org/english/
iran-increases-its-military-presence-security-official-shot-in-saqez

———, "Several Members of IRGC Killed or Injured Outside Rabat," June 25, 2015g. As of April 25, 2016:
http://pdki.org/english/several-irgc-killed-and-injured-outside-rabat

"Deputy PM Akdoğan Strikes Back at HDP, Calls It 'Extension' of PKK," *Hurriyet Daily News*, September 9, 2015. As of April 25, 2016:
http://www.hurriyetdailynews.com/deputy-pm-akdogan-strikes-back-at-hdp-calls-it-extension-of-pkk.aspx?pageID=238&nID=88261&NewsCatID=338

"Disarm or Leave Iraq' Says Iraq's Talabani to PKK," Reuters, March 24, 2009.

"Do Fa'aal-e Kargari Dar Sanandaj Baraye Tajamo-e Hemayat Az Kobani beh Habs va Shalagh Mahkoum Shodand [Two Labor Activists in Sanandaj Sentenced to Prison and Lashings for Protest in Support of Kobani]," BBC Persian, April 16, 2015. As of April 25, 2016:
http://www.bbc.co.uk/persian/iran/2015/04/150416_l45_sanandaj_activists

"Doktor Rouhani: Khaast-e Iran Hefz-e Yekparchegi va Vahdat-e Aragh Ast [Dr. Rouhani: Iran's Desire Is Preservation of Single, United Iraq]," Official Website of the President of the Islamic Republic of Iran, undated. As of April 25, 2016:
http://www.president.ir/fa/81340

Dombey, Daniel, "Turkey Ready to Accept Kurdish State in Historic Shift," *Financial Times*, June 27, 2014.

Dosky, Abdul-Khaleq, "Political or Economic? New Turkish-Kurdish Border Crossings Send Message to Baghdad," *Niqash*, March 20, 2014. As of April 25, 2016:
http://www.niqash.org/en/articles/economy/3403/

"Ellat-e Hemayat-e Ankara Az Esteghlaal-e Aghlim-e Kurdistan Chiist? [What Are Reasons Behind Turkey's Support for Kurdistan's Independence?]," *Mashregh News*, August 2, 2014.

Erkuş, Sevil, "Turkey Plans Iraq Camp to Prevent Refugee Flow," *Hurriyet Daily News*, August 5, 2014a.

———, "Turkish Army's Special Forces to Train Peshmerga," *Hurriyet Daily News*, November 21, 2014b.

"Esteghlaal-e Aghliim-e Kurdistan-e Aragh Dar Kootah Modat Namomken Ast [Independence of Iraq's Kurdish Region Not Possible in Short Term]," *Mashregh News*, July 22, 2014.

"Estemraar-e Koshteh Shodan-e Javanaan-e Kord Dar Fa'aaliatha-ye Nezami-ye Da'esh [Continuation of Kurdish Youth Deaths in ISIL Operations]," Kurdish Press News Agency, April 9, 2015.

"Etela'ie-ye Dabirkhane-ye Hezb-e Demokraat Darbare-ye Youresh beh Kamp-e Hezb-e Demokrat [KDPI Secretariat's Announcement Regarding Attack on KDPI's Camp]," *Kurdistan Media*, March 4, 2015.

"E'terazaat-e Rooz-e Kozashte-ye Shahrha-ye Kordestan [Yesterday's Protests in Kurdish Cities]," Kurdish Press News Agency, May 10, 2015.

Fevzi, Bilgin, and Ali Sarihan, eds., *Understanding Turkey's Kurdish Question*, Lanham, Md: Lexington Books, 2013.

Fielding-Smith, Abigail, "Turkey Finds a Gateway to Iraq," *Financial Times*, April 14, 2010.

Filkins, Dexter, "The Fight of Their Lives," *The New Yorker*, September 29, 2014.

Gafarli, Orhan, "Turkey's Tactical Rapprochement with Iraq and Iran," *Jamestown Foundation Eurasia Daily Monitor*, Vol. 12, No. 27, February 11, 2015.

Gordon, Michael R., and Bernard E Trainor, *Cobra II: The Inside Story of the Invasion and Occupation of Iraq*, New York: Knopf Doubleday Publishing Group, 2006.

———, *The Endgame: The Inside Story of the Struggle for Iraq, from George W. Bush to Barack Obama*, New York: Vintage Books, 2012.

"Gorran Forgets the 4th Anniversary of Feb 17 Uprising in Iraqi Kurdistan," *Ekurd Daily*, February 18, 2015.

Government of Iraq, "Iraqi Constitution," October 15, 2005. As of May 4, 2016: http://www.iraqinationality.gov.iq/attach/iraqi_constitution.pdf

Gözkaman, Armağan, "The Iraqi Conundrum: A Source of Insecurity for Turkey?" in Ebru Canan-Sokullu, ed., *Debating Security in Turkey: Challenges and Changes in the Twenty-First Century*, Lanham, Md.: Lexington Books, 2013.

Gunter, Michael M., "The KDP-PUK Conflict in Northern Iraq," *The Middle East Journal*, Vol. 50, No. 2, Spring 1996, pp. 224–241.

———, "The Continuing Kurdish Problem in Turkey After Öcalan's Capture," *Third World Quarterly*, Vol. 21, No. 5, 2000, pp. 849–869.

———, "The Five Stages of American Foreign Policy Toward the Kurds," *Insight Turkey,* Vol. 13, No. 2, 2011, pp. 93–106.

———, "The Kurdish Spring," *Third World Quarterly*, Vol. 34, No. 3, April 2013, pp. 441–457.

Gurcan, Metin, "Ankara Hardening Anti-PKK Strategy," *Al-Monitor*, September 12, 2016. As of September 27, 2016: http://www.al-monitor.com/pulse/originals/2016/09/turkey-new-anti-pkk-strategy.html

Gursel, Kadri, "Turkey's Emergency Rule Stokes Kurdish Separatism," Al-Monitor, September 13, 2016. As of September 27, 2016: http://www.al-monitor.com/pulse/originals/2016/09/turkey-emergency-rule-stokes-kurdish-separatism.html.

"Hamle-ye Nirooha-ye Amniyati be Tajamo-e Hemaayat az Kobani Dar Marivan [Security Forces in Marivan Attack Rally in Support of Kobani]," Human Rights Activists News Agency, October 8, 2014.

Harris, Winston, "Chaos in Iraq: Are the Kurds Truly Set to Win?" *Small Wars Journal*, Vol. 28, No. 9, 2014.

Hawramy, Fazel, "Border Smuggling Rises in Iranian Kurdistan," *Al-Monitor*, October 29, 2013.

Henley, Jon, Kareem Shaheen, and Constanze Letsch, "Turkey Election: Erdoğan and AKP Return to Power with Outright Majority," *The Guardian*, November 2, 2015.

Hiltermann, Joost R., "Revenge of the Kurds," *Foreign Affairs*, Vol. 91, No. 6, 2012, pp. 16–22.

"Hodood-e 300 Shahrvand-e Saghezi Tavasot-e Nirooha-ye Amniati Bazdaasht Shodand [Around 300 Residents of Saghez Arrested by Security Forces]," Kurdish Press News Agency, April 11, 2015.

Hoppe, Ralf, Maximilian Popp, Christoph Reuter, and Jonathan Stock, "New Alignments: The Kurds' Lonely Fight Against Islamic State," *Der Spiegel*, October 29, 2014.

"Hoshdaar-e Dabir Kol-e Asa'ib Ahl al-Haq Darbaare-ye Su' Estefaade-ye Kurdha-ye Aragh [Head of Asa'ib Ahl al-Haq's Warning About Iraq's Kurds Taking Advantage]," Ahlul Bayt News Agency, June 28, 2014.

"Hoshdar-e Amir-Abdollahian beh Saraan-e Kurdistan-e Aragh [Amir-Abdollahian's Warning to Leaders of Iraqi Kurdistan]," Fars News Agency, July 1, 2014.

"How Does the PUK-Gorran Deal Affect Kurdish Politics?" Rudaw, May 19, 2016. As of September 27, 2016: http://rudaw.net/english/kurdistan/19052016

Idiz, Semih, "Turkish Military Angered by Ankara's Peshmerga Move," *Al-Monitor*, October 31, 2014.

———, "Erdoğan Aims to Create Stronger Presidential System," *Al-Monitor*, February 3, 2015a.

———, "Erdoğan Continues to Stir the Pot in Turkey," *Al-Monitor*, September 8, 2015b. As of April 25, 2016: http://www.al-monitor.com/pulse/originals/2015/09/turkey-erdogan-continues-stir-cauldron-elections-pkk.html

International Crisis Group, "Iraq: Allaying Turkey's Fears over Kurdish Ambitions," Crisis Group Middle East, 2005.

International Middle East Peace Research Center, *Perception of Iranian Kurds Towards Turkey's Kurdish Question and Solution Process*, Ankara, Turkey, 2014.

Invest in Group, "Overview: Kurdistan Region—Economy," October 2013. As of April 25, 2016:
http://www.investingroup.org/publications/kurdistan/overview/economy/

"Iran Has Terrorized the Kurds Alliance," *Kurdish Info*, August 29, 2014.

"Iran Reveals It Is Negotiating with Its Rebel Kurdish Groups," *Rudaw*, September 12, 2014.

"Iran Worried by Kurdish Progress in the Region: KDPI," *Bas News*, December 15, 2015. As of April 25, 2016:
http://www.basnews.com/index.php/en/news/middle-east/248589

"Iran-Iraqi Kurdistan Region Annual Trade Hits $6bn," Islamic Republic News Agency, February 25, 2015.

"Iranian Army Shells Kandil Area," *Kurdish Info*, February 25, 2015. As of April 25, 2016:
http://www.kurdishinfo.com/iranian-army-shells-kandil-area

"Iranian Kurdish Group Shifts Policy, Seeking Democratic Autonomy," *Rudaw*, May 6, 2014.

"Iranian Kurdistan," The Hague, Netherlands: Unrepresented Nations and Peoples Organization, 2010.

"Iraq: Kurdish President Proposes Independence Referendum," *The Guardian*, July 3, 2014.

"Iraq Kurdistan Independence Referendum Planned," BBC News, July 1, 2014. As of May 4, 2016:
http://www.bbc.com/news/world-middle-east-28103124

"Iraqi Kurdistan: Gorran Movement Popularity Decreases After Deal with Barzani's KDP," *Ekurd Daily*, May 14, 2014.

"Iraqi Kurdistan Opens Official Crude Oil Trade Route via Iran," Reuters, August 7, 2013.

"Iraqi Kurds Send More Troops into Standoff with Iraq Army," Reuters, 2012.

"Iraq's Fugitive VP Not to Return to Iraq: Turkey," *China Daily USA*, September 11, 2012.

Izady, Mehrdad R., *The Kurds: A Concise Handbook*, Washington, D.C.: Taylor & Francis, 1992.

Jabary, Kawa, and Anil Hira, "The Kurdish Mirage: A Success Story in Doubt," *Middle East Policy*, Vol. 20, No. 2, Summer 2013, pp. 99–112.

Javedanfar, Meir, "Is Jalal Talabani's Patriotic Union of Kurdistan Another Iranian Ally in the Iraqi Government?" MEEPAS, 2005.

Jenkins, Gareth, "Turkey Rattles the Sabre over Kirkuk," *Al-Ahram*, No. 728, February 3–9, 2005.

———, "Turkey: AKP Pays the Price," International Relations and Security Network (ISN), April 1, 2009. As of April 25, 2016: http://www.isn.ethz.ch/Digital-Library/Articles/Detail/?id=98450

———, "Good Kurd, Bad Kurd: The AKP's Rapprochement with the KRG," *Turkey Analyst*, Vol. 6, No. 22, December 4, 2013.

———, "Yesterday's Wars: The Cause and Consequences of Turkish Inactions Against the Islamic State," *Turkey Analyst*, Vol. 7, No. 18, October 8, 2014.

Kane, Kevin, "How The Kurdistan Problem Could Torpedo the Iraq Energy Comeback," *Business Insider*, January 15, 2010.

Kane, Sean, *The Coming Turkish-Iranian Competition in Iraq*, Washington, D.C.: U.S. Institute for Peace, 2011.

"KCK: Iran Has Started a Dangerous Process," *Kurdish Info*, February 21, 2015. As of April 25, 2016: http://www.kurdishinfo.com/kck-iran-started-dangerous-process

Khalaji, Mehdi, *Salafism as a National Security Threat for Iran*, Washington, D.C.: Washington Institute for Near East Policy, 2014.

Khalil, Lydia, "The Hidden Hand of Iran in the Resurgence of Ansar Al-Islam," *Terrorism Monitor*, Vol. 5, No. 11, 2007.

Kinzer, Stephen, "Kurds Sense a Shift Toward Peace After 15-Year War," *New York Times*, November 27, 1999.

Kittleson, Shelly, "U.S., Iran Woo Rival Kurdish Factions in Battle Against IS," *Al-Monitor*, September 22, 2014.

Knights, Michael, "Making the Iraqi Revenue-Generating Deal Work," Washington Institute for Near East Policy, Policywatch 2341, December 3, 2014.

Knodell, Kevin, "Cleric's Murder Threatens to Blow Up Kurdish-Shia Alliance," *Medium*, December 28, 2014. As of May 4, 2016: https://medium.com/war-is-boring/murder-of-ethnic-kurdish-cleric-sparks-outrage-e99741e1c4d5

Komala Party of Iranian Kurdistan, "The Necessity of Changing the Political System of Government into a Federal Republic of States Komala," July 2001.

———, "KDPI-Komala Signed Memorandum of Agreement for Cooperation and Coordination," March 8, 2013.

"Koshteh Shodan-e Javanaan-e Manaateq-e Kordneshin-e Iran Dar Fa'aliatha-ye Nezami-ye Da'esh [Youths from Iranian Kurdish Regions Killed in ISIL Military Activities]," *Kurdane*, January 19, 2015.

Kottasova, Ivana "How Turkey Turned from Emerging Star to Economic Mess," CNN.com, August 7, 2014. As of April 25, 2016: http://edition.cnn.com/2014/08/07/business/turkey-economy-problems/

Kucuksahin, Sukru, "Kurds Become New Target of Ankara's Post-Coup Purges," *Al-Monitor,* September 12, 2016. As of September 27, 2016: http://www.al-monitor.com/pulse/originals/2016/09/ turkey-kurds-become-new-target-of-post-coup-purges.html

"Kurdish History and Language According to Iran Draws KRG Protest," *Rudaw*, May 15, 2014.

"Kurdish Oil Exports Add Tensions to Iraq," *Energy Tribune*, June 1, 2009.

"Kurdish Troops Seize Iraq's Kirkuk, Bai Hassan Oilfields," NBC Newsroom, July 11, 2014. As of May 4, 2016: http://www.nbcnews.com/storyline/iraq-turmoil/ kurdish-troops-seize-iraqs-kirkuk-bai-hassan-oilfields-n153481

"Kurdistan Negotiating Gas and Oil Deals with Iran," *Kurdish Globe*, March 2, 2015.

Kurdistan Regional Government, "Oil and Gas Law of the Kurdistan Region–Iraq," 2007.

Kurdistan Regional Government, Ministry of Natural Resources, *Oil Production, Export, and Consumption Report 2015*, Erbil, 2016. As of May 23, 2016: http://mnr.krg.org/images/monthlyreports/KRG_MNR_Full_Annual_ Report_2015_2.pdf

Kurdistan Regional Government Cabinet, "Ministry of Natural Resources Announces Start of Crude Oil Exports from Kurdistan Region, Iraq," 2009.

Kurdistan Regional Government Department of Foreign Relations, "Kurdistan Regional Government," 2016. As of April 26, 2016: http://dfr.gov.krd/p/p.aspx?p=88&l=12&s=030400&r=403

"Kurds to Be Removed from Kirkuk over Turkey Anger," *Irish Times*, April 10, 2003.

Kuru, Ahmet T., "Turkey, Iran, and the Sunni-Shiite Tension," *Today's Zaman*, October 4, 2012.

Kutschera, Chris, "Have the Kurds Lost the Battle for Kirkuk?" *Middle East*, No. 383, 2007, pp. 10–12.

"Kuzey Irak'tan Ham Petrol Akışı Yükseldi," *Fortune Turkey*, January 14, 2015.

Lake, Eli, "Kurdish Protectors Vow to Keep Their 'Jerusalem,'" *Bloomberg View*, January 27, 2015.

"Lally Weymouth Interviews Former Iraqi Foreign Minister Hoshyar Zebari," *Washington Post*, August 12, 2014. As of April 25, 2016: http://www.washingtonpost.com/world/middle_east/lally-weymouth-interviews-former-iraqi-foreign-minister-hoshyar-zebari/2014/08/12/98f4a838-2257-11e4-8593-da634b334390_story.html

Larrabee, F. Stephen, *Troubled Partnership: U.S.-Turkish Relations in an Era of Global Geopolitical Change*, Santa Monica, Calif.: RAND Corporation, MG-899-AF, 2010. As of May 4, 2016: http://www.rand.org/pubs/monographs/MG899.html

———, "Turkey's New Kurdish Opening," *Survival: Global Politics and Strategy*, Vol. 55, No. 5, 2013, pp. 133–146.

Larrabee, F. Stephen, and Gönül Tol, "Turkey's Kurdish Challenge," *Survival: Global Politics and Strategy*, Vol. 53, No. 4, 2011, pp. 143–152.

League of Nations, "Covenant of the League of Nations," April 28, 1919.

Lekic, Slobodan, "Sykes-Picot Agreement: Line in the Sand Still Shapes Middle East," *Stars and Stripes*, June 19, 2014. As of May 5, 2016: http://www.stripes.com/news/sykes-picot-agreement-line-in-the-sand-still-shapes-middle-east-1.289723

Letsch, Constanze, and Ian Traynor, "Turkey Election: Ruling Party Loses Majority as Pro-Kurdish HDP Gains Seats," *The Guardian*, June 7, 2015.

MacDiarmid, Campbell, "Kurds Rail Against Government Corruption as Protests Turn Violent in Iraqi Kurdistan," *International Business Times*, October 16, 2015.

"Maghaam-e Kurdistan-e Aragh Dar Mowred-e Hamkari-ye Shebe Nezamiaan-e Shi'a ba Artesh Hoshdaar Daad [KRG Official Warns of Shi'a Militant Cooperation with Military]," BBC Persian, 2015. As of April 25, 2016: http://www.bbc.co.uk/persian/world/2015/03/150317_l03_iraq_is_iran

Malik, Kenan, "As Old Orders Crumble, Progressive Alternatives Struggle to Emerge," *The Guardian*, June 13, 2015.

"Massoud Barzani: Hich Rokhdaadi Maane'ye Esteghlaal-e Kurdistan as Aragh Nemishavad [Massoud Barzani: Nothing Will Get in the Way of Kurdistan's Independence from Iraq]," *Voice of America*, April 20, 2015.

McDowall, David, *Modern History of the Kurds*, New York: I.B. Tauris, 2003.

Mir-Hosseini, Ziba, "Inner Truth and Outer History: The Two Worlds of the Ahl-i Haqq of Kurdistan," *International Journal of Middle East Studies*, Vol. 26, No. 2, 1994, p. 267.

"Most Turks See Erdoğan as Culprit in Failure of Coalition Talks," *Hurriyet Daily News*, August 28, 2015. As of April 25, 2016:
http://www.hurriyetdailynews.com/most-turks-see-Erdoğan-as-culprit-in-failure-of-coalition-talks-poll.aspx?pageID=238&nID=87648&NewsCatID=338

Nader, Alireza, *Iran's Role in Iraq: Room for U.S.-Iran Cooperation?* Santa Monica, Calif.: RAND Corporation, PE-151-OSD, 2015. As of May 4, 2016:
http://www.rand.org/pubs/perspectives/PE151.html

Namazi, Marjan, "Iran Fears an Independent Kurdistan in Iraq," *Iran Wire*, August 6, 2014.

Natali, Denise, *The Kurds and the State: Evolving National Identity in Iraq, Turkey, and Iran*, Syracuse, N.Y.: Syracuse University Press, 2005.

———, "The Kirkuk Conundrum," *Ethnopolitics*, Vol., 7, No. 4, 2008, pp. 433–443.

———, *The Kurdish Quasi-State: Development and Dependency in Post–Gulf War Iraq*, Syracuse, N.Y.: Syracuse University Press, 2010.

———, "Turkey's Kurdish Client State," *Al-Monitor*, November 14, 2014.

Natali, Denise, Daniel Serwer, Mohammed Shareef, and Gönül Tol, "Panel Discussion: The Kurds' New Clout in U.S. Ties with Turkey and Iraq," Middle East Institute, Washington, D.C., May 1, 2015.

O'Byrne, David, "Turkey's Kurdish Party Under Attack," *Financial Times*, September 10, 2015. As of April 25, 2016:
http://www.ft.com/intl/cms/s/0/5d84c260-57d0-11e5-9846-de406ccb37f2.html#axzz3mgPZXj9R

Organisation for Economic Co-operation and Development, "Domestic Product," undated. As of May 4, 2016:
https://data.oecd.org/gdp/gross-domestic-product-gdp.htm

Osgood, Patrick, "In Payment Drought, Oil Companies Pare KRG Investment," *Iraq Oil Report*, February 10, 2015.

Osgood, Patrick, and Rawaz Tahir, "KRG Receives First 2015 Budget Payment," *Iraq Oil Report*, May 4, 2015.

Ottaway, Marina, and David Ottaway, "How the Kurds Got Their Way," *Foreign Affairs*, Vol. 93, No. 3, May/June 2014.

Pamuk, Humeyra, and Orhan Coskun, "Exclusive: Turkey, Iraqi Kurdistan Clinch Major Energy Pipeline Deals," Reuters, November 6, 2013. As of April 5, 2016:
http://www.reuters.com/article/us-turkey-iraq-kurdistan-idUSBRE9A50HR20131106

Park, Bill, *Turkey-Kurdish Regional Government Relations After the U.S. Withdrawal from Iraq: Putting the Kurds on the Map?* Carlisle, Pa.: U.S. Army War College Press, 2014.

Parker, Ned, Babak Dehghanpisheh, and Isabel Coles, "How Iran's Military Chiefs Operate in Iraq," Reuters, February 24, 2015.

Pashang, Ardeshir, "Iran va Masale-i Benaam-e Esteghlaal-e Ehtemaali-ye Kordestan-e Aragh [Iran and an Issue Called the Likely Independence of Iraq's Kurdistan]," *IR Diplomacy*, August 3, 2014.

Paul, Amanda, and Demir Murat Seyrek, "Turkey's New Election: War or Peace?" *Al-Jazeera*, October 30, 2015. As of April 4, 2016:
http://www.aljazeera.com/indepth/opinion/2015/10/
turkey-election-war-peace-151028093829631.html

Peker, Emre, and Yeliz Candemir, "Turkey's 2014 GDP Below Official Expectations," *Wall Street Journal*, March 31, 2015.

Pirog, Robert, "Memorandum: Kurdish Oil Exports and U.S. Policy," Washington, D.C.: Congressional Research Service, September 10, 2014.

"PKK Blocks KDPI Convoy as Inter-Kurdish Conflict Continues," *Rudaw*, May 26, 2015.

Pollack, David, "Will Iraq's Crisis Lead to Kurdistan's Independence?" *Fikra Forum*, July 1, 2014. As of May 4, 2016:
http://fikraforum.org/?p=5066#.VypX-XCs188

"Press Conference by Turkish Prime Minister Ahmet Davutoğlu and KRG President Masoud Barzani," 4:30 and 9:20, Erbil, 2014.

"Purges Since Coup Attempt in Turkey Shake Higher Education," Reuters, August 30, 2016. As of September 19, 2016:
http://www.voanews.com/a/purges-since-coup-attempt-turkey-shake-higher-education/3487226.html

Qader, Histyar, "In Northern Iraq, a Sign of the Civil War to Come?" *Niqash*, November 26, 2015. As of April 25, 2016:
http://www.niqash.org/en/articles/security/5162

Qadir, Hazhar Jabar, "ISIL's Wave on Reshaping Turkish Foreign Policy Towards Iraqi Kurdistan," *Bas News*, January 18, 2015.

Qurbani, Arif, "Kurds in the New Shiite-Sunni Game," *Rudaw*, April 6, 2015.

Razzouk, Nayla, "Iraq's Kurds to Start Natural Gas Exports to Turkey in 2019–2020," Bloomberg, January 15, 2016. As of May 4, 2016:
http://www.bloomberg.com/news/articles/2016-01-15/
iraq-s-kurds-to-start-natural-gas-exports-to-turkey-in-2019-2020

"Record Growth at Erbil International Airport," *Iraq Business News*, January 23, 2013.

Reilly, Patrick, "The Election of the Middle East," *The Gate*, May 25, 2015. As of April 25, 2016:
http://uchicagogate.com/2015/05/25/the-election-of-the-middle-east/

Republic of Turkey, Ministry of Foreign Affairs, "Policy of Zero Problems with our Neighbors," web page, undated-a. As of April 25, 2016: http://www.mfa.gov.tr/policy-of-zero-problems-with-our-neighbors.en.mfa

———, "Turkey's Energy Profile and Strategy," web page, undated-b. As of April 4, 2016: http://www.mfa.gov.tr/turkeys-energy-strategy.en.mfa

Richards, George, "Across the Zagros: Iranian Influence in Iraqi Kurdistan," *The Guardian*, November 21, 2013.

Ricotta, Jill, "Turkey: Parliamentary Elections and Their Aftermath," webcast summary, Woodrow Wilson International Center for Scholars, June 9, 2015. As of September 29, 2015: https://www.wilsoncenter.org/event/turkey-parliamentary-elections-and-their-aftermath#sthash.PNT8H9sg.dpuf

Ridha, Haywa, "Thanks to Nuclear Deal, Iranian Migrant Workers Plan to Leave Iraq," *Niqash*, April 30, 2015.

Saadullah, Vager, "Iranian Peshmerga Chief: Iran Set Ambushes for Us," *Al-Monitor*, October 14, 2014.

Sadiq, Hoshmand, "Clashes Between PKK and KDPI Continue," *Bas News*, May 24, 2015.

"Safar-e Vazir Khareje-ye Amrika va Tote'e-ye Tajzie-ye Aragh [U.S. Secretary of State's Visit and Conspiracy to Split Up Iraq]," Islamic Republic News Agency, June 25, 2014.

Safire, William, "Getting on with It," *New York Times*, March 17, 2003.

Salama, Vivian, and Bram Janssen, "Uneasy Alliance of Kurds, Shiites Formed in Northern Iraq," Associated Press, February 17, 2015.

Salih, Hemin, "KDP Follows U.S. Lead, Improves Relations with Iran," *Bas News*, January 20, 2015a.

———, "Goran Leader Rejects Qassem Suleimani's Request," *Bas News*, April 1, 2015b.

Salih, Mohammed A., "Kurds Reject Proposed Rival Force in Kirkuk," *Al-Monitor*, February 12, 2015a.

———, "KRG Seeks $5 Billion Lifeline," *Al-Monitor*, June 23, 2015b. As of May 4, 2016: http://www.al-monitor.com/pulse/originals/2015/06/iraq-kurdistan-government-loans-international-banks.html

Salman, Raheem, and Mustafa Mahmoud, "Kurds Seize Iraq Oilfields, Ministers Pull Out of Government," Reuters, July 11, 2014.

Satana, Nil S., "Civilianization of Politics in Turkey," Middle East Institute, April 16, 2014. As of April 25, 2016:
http://www.mei.edu/content/civilianization-politics-turkey

Scotten, Ali, "Are Islamic State Militants Operating Inside Iran?" Scotten Consulting, September 7, 2014.

Sheppard, David, "With New Grip on Oil Fields, Iraq Kurds Unveil Plan to Ramp Up Exports," Reuters, June 26, 2014.

Shields, Sarah, "Mosul, the Ottoman Legacy and the League of Nations," *International Journal of Contemporary Iraqi Studies*, Vol. 3, No. 2, October 2009, pp. 217–230.

Smith, Daniel W., and staff, "Kurdistan Budget Payment Imminent," *Iraq Oil Report*, February 11, 2015.

"Sobhani, Mohammad Ali, "Kodam Aragh Manafe-ye Iran ra Ta'miin Mikonad? [Which Iraq Will Secure Iran's Interests?]," *Hamshahri*, April 28, 2008.

Stansfield, Gareth, "Kurdistan Rising: To Acknowledge or Ignore the Unraveling of Iraq," in *Middle East Memo*, Washington, D.C.: Brookings Institution, 2014.

Stansfield, Gareth, and Liam Anderson, "Kurds in Iraq: The Struggle Between Baghdad and Erbil," *Middle East Policy*, Vol. 16, No. 1, Spring 2009, pp. 134–145.

Statistical Center of Iran, *Nataayej-e Amaar-Giri-ye Niiroy-e Kaar: Tabestaan 1393 [Labor Force Statistics: Summer 1393]*, Tehran, 2014.

Stewart, Richard Winship, *American Military History,* Volume II: *The United States Army in a Global Era, 1917–2008*, Washington, D.C.: U.S. Government Printing Office, 2010.

Strakes, Jason E., "Current Political Complexities of the Iraqi Turkmen," *Iran and the Caucasus*, Vol. 13, No. 2, 2009, pp. 365–382.

Stratfor Global Intelligence, "Turkey: Iraq's Turkmen and Kurds," Austin, Tex., March 3, 2008.

Sullivan, Marisa, *Maliki's Authoritarian Regime*, Washington, D.C.: Institute for the Study of War, April 20, 2013.

Tahir, Rawaz, and Patrick Osgood, "UPDATE: Baghdad-Erbil Cooperation Fraying," *Iraq Oil Report*, January 29, 2015.

"Tahlil-e Raftari-ye Kurdha-ye Aragh [Behavioral Analysis of Iraq's Kurds]," *Mashregh News*, June 30, 2014.

"Tajamo-e Mo'tarezaan Dar Mahabad Beh Khoshoonat Keshideh Shodeh [Protest in Mahabad Turns Violent]," BBC Persian, May 7, 2015. As of April 25, 2016:
http://www.bbc.co.uk/persian/
iran/2015/05/150507_l45_mahabad_rape_allegation_demo

"Tajzie-ye Aragh: Sood Ya Zian-e Iran? [Partition of Iraq: Iran's Benefit or Loss?]," *Rahesabz*, October 22, 2014.

Tanchum, Micha'el, "The Kurds' Big Year," *Foreign Affairs*, Vol. 94, No. 1, January 12, 2015a.

———, "The Kurdish Consolidation," *Foreign Affairs*, June 29, 2015b.

"Tanesh va Na-araami dar Oshnavieh [Tensions and Unrest in Oshnavieh]," Kurdish Press Agency, May 28, 2015. As of April 25, 2016: http://www.kurdpa.net/farsi/idame/65187

Taşpinar, Ömer, and Gönül Tol, *Turkey and the Kurds: From Predicament to Opportunity*, Washington, D.C.: Brookings Center on the United States and Europe, 2014.

Taştekin, Fehim, "Turkey's Sunni Identity Test," *Al-Monitor*, June 21, 2013.

———, "Iraqi Turkmen Feel Abandoned by Turkey," *Al-Monitor*, June 20, 2014.

Tharoor, Ishaan, "Turkey's Election Deepens Erdogan Hold on Power amid Regional Crises," *Washington Post*, November 2, 2015.

Tocci, Nathalie, "Turkey's Kurdish Gamble," *The International Spectator*, Vol. 48, No. 3, 2013.

Tohidi, Nayereh, "Ethnicity and Religious Minority Politics in Iran," in Ali Gheissari, ed., *Contemporary Iran: Economy, Society, Politics*, New York: Oxford University Press, 2009, pp. 299–323.

Tol, Gönül, "A New Era in Turkey's Civil-Military Relations," Middle East Institute, August 30, 2010. As of May 4, 2016: http://www.mei.edu/content/new-era-turkeys-civil-military-relations

———, "Turkey's KRG Energy Partnership," *Foreign Policy*, January 29, 2013.

———, "Ankara's Influence over Barzani Wanes," *Al-Monitor*, December 10, 2014.

———, "Erdoğan's High-Risk Strategy," Middle East Institute, August 6, 2015a. As of April 25, 2016: http://www.mei.edu/content/article/Erdoğan%E2%80%99s-high-risk-strategy

———, "Turkey's Risky War with the Kurds," Middle East Institute, September 17, 2015b. As of May 4, 2016: http://www.mei.edu/content/article/turkey%E2%80%99s-risky-war-kurds

Trompiz, Gus, and Anna Driver, "Iraq Says Exxon Mobil Freezes Kurdistan Deal," Reuters, March 16, 2012.

"Turkey, Iraq Pledge More Military Cooperation in Fight Against Islamic State," *International Business Times*, December 26, 2014.

"Turkey Rejects Independent Kurdish State, Wants Iraq Unity Government," Reuters, June 30, 2014.

"Turkey 'Targets PYD, Not Kurds' in Syria," *Hurriyet Daily News*, August 31, 2016. As of September 15, 2016:
http://www.hurriyetdailynews.com/turkey-targets-pyd-not-kurds-in-syria.aspx?pageID=238&nID=103436&NewsCatID=352

"Turkey's AKP Spokesman: Iraq's Kurds Have Right to Decide Their Future," *Rudaw*, 2014.

"Turkey to Allow 200 Peshmerga Fighters Passage to Kobani," Radio Free Europe/Radio Liberty, October 23, 2014. As of April 25, 2016:
http://www.rferl.org/content/turkey-iraq-syria-kogani-kurds/26652368.html

"Turkey Wants to Open Consulate Offices in Kirkuk and Basra," *BasNews*, May 22, 2015.

Turkish Consulate General in Erbil, "Consulate General's Message," undated-a. As of April 25, 2016:
http://erbil.bk.mfa.gov.tr/AmbassadorsMessage.aspx

———, "Mission," undated-b. As of April 25, 2016:
http://erbil.bk.mfa.gov.tr/Mission.aspx

"Tuz Khurmatu Turkmen Take Up Arms in Fight Against ISIL," *Anadolu Agency*, June 17, 2014.

United Nations Security Council, *Resolution 688: Iraq*, New York, 1991.

"Up to 18 Killed in Tuz Khurmatu Violence," *NRT*, November 17, 2015. As of April 25, 2016:
http://nrttv.com/EN/Details.aspx?Jimare=4110

U.S. Energy Information Administration, "Iraq," undated. As of April 25, 2016:
http://www.eia.gov/countries/cab.cfm?fips=IZ

Van Heuvelen, Ben, and Ben Lando, "Analysis: Iraq's Oil Disputes Remain Unresolved," *Iraq Oil Report*, December 10, 2014.

Van Heuvelen, Ben, Ben Lando, and Patrick Osgood, "U.S. Court Takes on Iraq Oil Dispute," *Iraq Oil Report*, January 9, 2015.

Van Wilgenburg, Wladimir, "Iranian Kurdish Parties Prefer Dialogue with Government," *Al-Monitor*, January 14, 2014.

———, "In Kobani, Some Kurds Were Fighting Kurds," *Medium*, January 9, 2015. As of May 4, 2016:
https://medium.com/@vvanwilgenburg/in-kobani-some-kurds-were-fighting-kurds-422511f387d2

Vatanka, Alex, "Why Iran Fears an Independent Kurdistan," *National Interest*, July 25, 2014.

Vatanka, Alex, and Sarkawt Shamsulddin, "Forget ISIS: Shia Militias Are the Real Threat to Kurdistan," *The National Interest*, January 7, 2015.

Voller, Yaniv, "Kurdish Oil Politics in Iraq: Contested Sovereignty and Unilateralism," *Middle East Policy*, Vol. 20, No. 1, Spring 2013, pp. 68–82.

Werz, Michael, and Max Hoffman, *The United States, Turkey, and the Kurdish Regions: The Peace Process in Context*, Washington, D.C.: Center for American Progress, 2014.

"Will Arming Peshmerga Tip Balance of Power in Iraq?" *Al-Hayat*, October 8, 2014.

Wilson, Woodrow, 14 Points speech, delivered before Congress, January 8, 1918.

World Bank, *The Kurdistan Region of Iraq: Assessing the Economic and Social Impact of the Syrian Conflict and ISIS*, Washington, D.C., 2015. As of April 4, 2016: http://elibrary.worldbank.org/doi/pdf/10.1596/978-1-4648-0548-6

Yezdani, İpek "Turkmens, Yazidis Flee Fearing Jihadist Push," *Hurriyet Daily News*, August 7, 2014.

Yildiz, Kerim, and Tanyel B. Taysi, *The Kurds in Iran: The Past, Present and Future*, London: Pluto, in association with Kurdish Human Rights Project, 2007.

Zaman, Amberin, "Turkish Kurds' Electoral Strategy Is a High-Wire Act," *Al-Monitor*, January 14, 2015a.

———, "Iran's Kurds Rise Up as Their Leaders Remain Divided," *Al-Monitor*, May 11, 2015b.

———, "For Turkey, Which Is the Lesser Evil: ISIS or the Kurds?" Woodrow Wilson International Center for Scholars, March 4, 2016a. As of September 19, 2016: https://www.wilsoncenter.org/publication/ for-turkey-which-the-lesser-evil-isis-or-the-kurds

———, *From Tribe to Nation: Iraqi Kurdistan on the Cusp of Statehood*, Washington, D.C.: Woodrow Wilson International Center for Scholars, Fall 2016b. As of September 27, 2016: https://www.wilsoncenter.org/sites/default/files/from_tribe_to_nation_final.pdf

Zambelis, Chris, "The Factors Behind Rebellion in Iranian Kurdistan," *Combating Terrorism Center Sentinel*, Vol. 4, No. 3, March 2011, pp. 18–21.

Zangeneh, Mohamed, "Turkish Sources Confirm Oil Export Deal with Kurdistan Region," *Asharq al-Awsat*, December 1, 2013.

Zaraei, Mohammad, "Roykard Regim-e Sahionisti beh Aragh-e Jadid [Zionist Regime's Approach to a New Iraq]," Fars News Agency, February 15, 2015.

Zeidan, Salam, "Turkey Pushing for Own 'Popular Mobilization' Militia in Iraqm," *Al-Akhbar English* (Lebanon), March 4, 2015.

Zulal, Shwan, "Reforming Iraqi Kurdistan's Oil Revenue," Carnegie Endowment for International Peace, 2011.